# A JOURNEY TO THE END OF THE EARTH

Storms, ice, snow and frozen Arctic seas
**THEN THERE WAS THE ENEMY!**

# WW2 NAVAL WARGAMES IN THE FROZEN NORTH

*A WW2 Convoy battle generator including Rules for resolving the battles*

*By* **MAL WRIGHT**

Nimble Books LLC

1521 Martha Avenue

Ann Arbor, MI, USA 48103

http://www.NimbleBooks.com

wfz@nimblebooks.com

+1.734-330-2593

Copyright 2010 by Mal Wright

Version 1.0; last saved 2010-09-02.

Printed in the United States of America

ISBN-13: 978-1-60888-006-5

The paper used in this publication meets the minimum requirements of the American National Standard for Information Sciences—Permanence of Paper for Printed Library Materials, ANSI Z39.48-1992. The paper is acid-free and lignin-free.

# A Journey to the end of the earth

### SURFACE SCALE.
Players should adjust the ground scale to suit their playing area. However I suggest the following, which my group have used with great success over the years, for use with a 3-minute move.
**20cm or 8 inches per nautical mile. At this scale 1cm = One knot. Therefore a ship moving at 20 knots can move 20cm.**
**2"(5cm) = 500 nautical yards. A ship moving at 14 knots moves 14cm and so forth.**

The scale used on the playing area is for the convenience of the players and can depend a lot on the size of the models in use. I use 1:3000 scale models almost exclusively, so my scales are well suited for them. In the case of 1:6000 scale ships.

### RANGES WITHIN THE RULES.
To allow players complete flexibility, <u>all ranges in these rules are quoted in Nautical Miles, or yards.</u> This avoids the need for players to make awkward conversions to the above three suggested ground scales.
I quote ranges. I have left it to you to choose the actual ground scale you choose.

The Commodore's flagship

WW2 Convoys to Russia. Master Map. © Mal. Wright. 2008

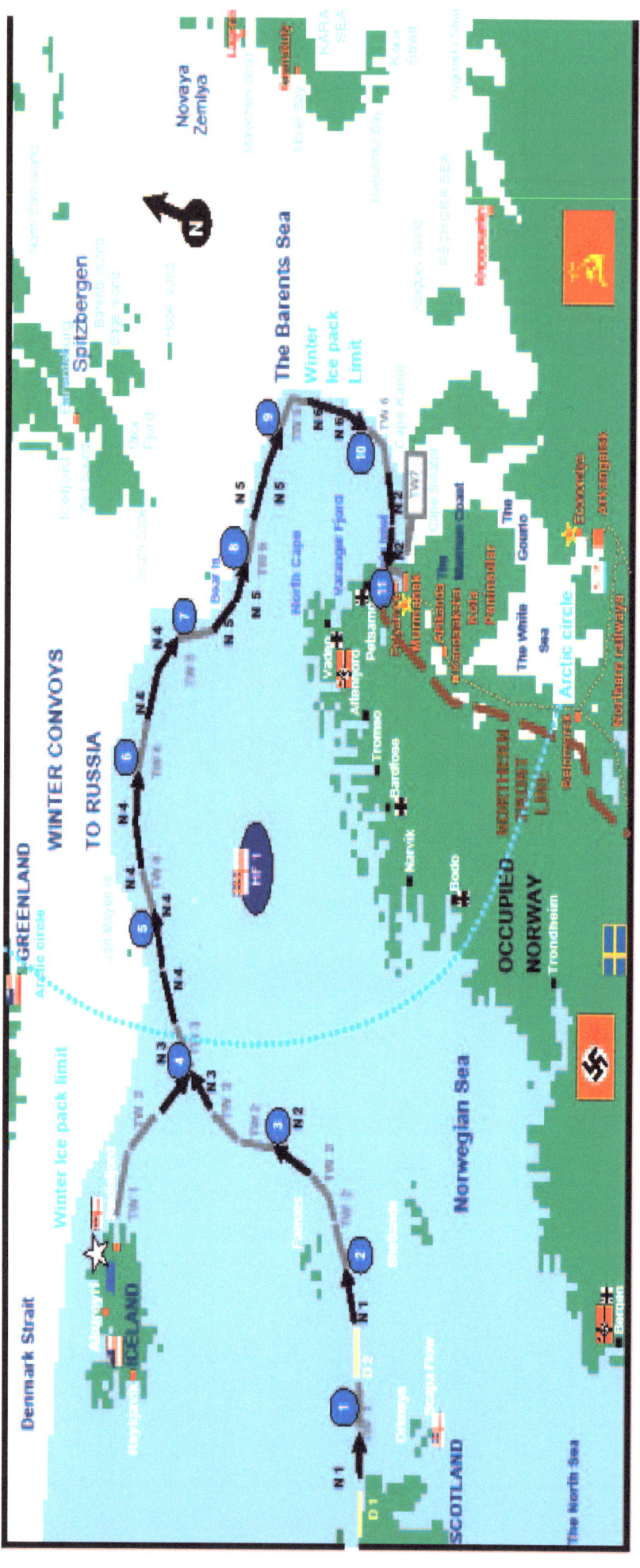

ARCTIC STORM. WW2 Winter Convoys to Russia. © Mal. Wright. 2008

WW2 Convoys to Russia. Summer Map. © Mal. Wright. 2009

## DEDICATION

This volume is dedicated to the memory of my Uncle Bert Taylor. He was only on one operation up into the Arctic, but that was apparently more than enough for a man who came from a warm country like Australia. He was sunk three times during WW2 but fortunately always in warm waters and survived to live well into retirement. His service and that of so many others helped to create a prosperous post war era.

## THANKS

I would like to thank all those naval wargamers who have gamed with me, corresponded, assisted with research, and generally made themselves helpful over a period of many years. They come from a wide range of nationalities and all corners of the earth. Their ideas have always been welcome and their input always valuable. Some have been nothing short of inspirational with their eagerness to see this volume in print. During a recent illness it was overwhelming and humbling to receive so many wishes of good will from all over the world. Thank you. I hope that this game pleases you all and at least partly repays you for your wonderful support.

SPECIAL MENTION

Many thanks to Dave Schueler, Andy Doty, and Gregory Kuntz

# A JOURNEY TO THE END OF THE EARTH

Even to the Russians, a hardy race with much experience at living in a cold land, swept by bitter winters, the Kola Peninsular and the Murman coast represented the very extreme of a distant, harsh and God forsaken place. Hence, they named their first colony there Murmansk. The end of the Earth:

To the Allied sailors of many nations who sailed there during WW2 it certainly seemed to live up to its name. Getting there was bad enough with all the hardships of freezing cold conditions, massive storms, and seas that could swallow up a ship leaving little trace. If forced to abandon ship in such waters they were under no illusions that they chances of survival were slim. There were some remarkable stories of survival but the privations endured by those who made it back alive were just as remarkable in that there were so few who lived to tell the tale of being sunk on the Murmansk run.

Of course, although the port facilities available were Spartan and poorly equipped to handle the huge amount of stores delivered, then there was the problem of getting such cargoes there in the first place.

Having arrived, there were almost no amenities for the crews of ships to use in order to rest up after fighting there way to Murmansk. Indeed the Soviets were reluctant to give the crews much freedom to go ashore at all. Food was scarce. That supplied was grudgingly given, boring and lacking nutrition. So for those who had arrived, the long wait until they could join a convoy back to the UK was like a prison sentence. Perhaps the only thing the Russians seemed to have plenty of was Vodka and with that they could be extremely generous.

## THE SOVIET SITUATION

Prior to WW2 the huge Soviet Nation was a state boasted of by the Communists and thought to be a workers utopia by western workers. But to governments of most other nations the Soviets were not to be trusted and their threats of expanding communism to the entire world were feared. The USSR was a vast nation about which little was really known.

Internal security was taken to extremes by the Soviets and the true brutality of the regime hidden from the West. Her people endured as much brutality under Stalin as they would later suffer from the Nazi invasion, but it was kept secret and those in the know refused to speak out for fear they would become the next victims of a repressive regime. Indeed one did not even need to speak out or oppose Stalin. It only need that it be suspected for the secret police to make arrests.

As a result of these purges the military forces of the Soviet Union suffered a crisis of leadership when Germany invaded in 1941. The Red Navy was not spared either and there was a serious lack of qualified officers. Commissars watched over every aspect of service, especially the decisions taken. Under such close and dangerous surveillance, those charged with making decisions tended toward caution. They suspected their senior officers and suspected their juniors lest they be blamed for mistakes.

When war required decision making, it was often taken in a manner that frustrated their Allies, who were used to being able to make decisive decisions without fear of those looking over their shoulder.

The Soviet Navy entered the war with a collection of very old ships and was in the early stages of building a more modern fleet. A canal between the Baltic and the White Sea enabled some movement of ships between those two areas. If conditions were right there could also be summer transfers between the Pacific and the Murman region via the Northern waterway across the top of Asia and Europe.

But large ships in the Baltic were trapped in those waters as were those of the Black Sea Fleet. Large ships were very few in the Pacific, therefore when the Northern area rose to prominence there was little that could be done to reinforce it with anything larger than destroyers.

At various times Soviet warships took part in these operations. Older and newer types of destroyers came out to meet the inbound convoys a few days from their destination. Similarly they helped take outbound convoys out for a few days as a local escort much as done at the other end from Scotland. The effectiveness of these ships was very limited at first. They lacked radar, sonar and the crews were poorly trained. But as time went by they were upgraded with Allied equipment. Sea time soon added experience as well, and the AA firepower most could put up, was always welcome.

Thus when Russia sought help in the form of war materials from its new Allies, the Red Navy was not in a position to be of much help. So it was that the convoys of merchant ships that were assembled and sent to the northern ports of the USSR were almost completely escorted by ships of the other Allies, with the bulk of this falling upon the British. Even the little help that was given was sparing, unreliable, and grudgingly given due to great suspicion with which the Communists saw in the Western powers.

Communist suspicion of the west was such that, the repair facilities present were at first denied to Allied ships. This later eased, but what was available was quite inadequate for the task. Materials and equipment for repair were in short supply and skilled workers had been sent off to fight at the front.

Murmansk was also close to the northern front line where German alpine troops and the Finns were attempting to close the port through its capture. Having failed to do that, they established air bases a short flight from Murmansk and tried to batter it to bits. At any one time, those who reached the port, could find themselves under intense air attack, as well as the frequent alarms when the Germans launched yet another offensive in an attempt to at least cut the railway line.

Murmansk had never been envisaged as a major port, therefore it was serviced by only a single railway line, which itself was in range of the Luftwaffe. Sections had been captured but the Soviets built a bypass to enable it to keep operating. None the less it remained a fragile link with the center of the country. Minesweeping capability was poor. Fuel storage was lacking.

Air attacks against ships after they had arrived, were frequent. But after an initial poor start; the Soviet's quickly increased the flak capability around Murmansk in particular. By 1943 this is described by allied observers as intense and very heavy. It no doubt has something to do with the decline of German success as time wore on.

During the summer months shipping could use the much better facilities at the port of Archangelsk. This was also much further away from the front line and had a good rail link to the rest of Russia. Anchorage area was quite adequate and warehousing was available.

Unfortunately Archangelsk could only be reached during the very weather which provided the best operating conditions for the Luftwaffe. If ships were caught there by winter they would be iced in and could not be released until the following spring. Such a waste of shipping was something Allies could do without, as they needed every hull that could carry war materials and other supplies to the vast number of ports demanding them.

The Admiralty preferred supply through Persia and the Pacific. The former was little opposed. The latter was possible because Japan was not at war with the Soviet Union until the last few days of WW2. Ships could convey vast amounts of material direct into Russian waters and they would not be interfered with by Japan. The full extent of Japanese reluctance to become involved in a war with the Soviets was little understood until after world war two. Therefore it was feared that if she did commence hostilities with the struggling Russians, as Germany was urging, that route would be easily cut. It was also at the end of an extremely long overland rail journey almost the length of Russia.

Axis armies were pressing on toward the eastern and southern provinces of the USSR. This posed the possibility that a victory in the Caucasus would cut the relatively easy route through Persia. In addition, while invaluable for supplying the more southerly fronts of the great struggle, supplies from the Persian route had to pass north across Russia and as such were open to loss from air attack and German land advances.

Using this argument, Stalin insisted that in order to supply his northern front, particularly around Leningrad, it was necessary for the Allies to send war material, food and fuel in via Murmansk.

## THE GERMAN SITUATION

The German capture of Norway in 1940 meant that any shipping that did move up the Norwegian Sea would have to pass within range of numerous Luftwaffe air bases. Some air flights by reconnaissance aircraft were long, but most attack flights were relatively short.

The Kriegsmarine also established submarine bases along the coast and the deep fjords were perfect shelter for heavy ships of the German navy. In some places a convoy would have to pass within a mere hour or so flying time of well established air bases and in addition such close proximity to the convoy routes meant warships could dart out, attack and retire without having to spend long periods at sea. This was important to the Kriegsmarine as from time to time it experienced serious fuel problems.

Land bases also provided a higher level of comforts and recreation facilities, which even if not completely satisfactory, were at least available in some form or other. Naval operations were brief and the time spent at sea therefore more tolerable than the Allies experienced.

Even though the range of Allied bombers increased as the war progressed, the Germans were able to move further north, keeping outside the range of attack, other than by special means. The distance attackers needed to travel also gave them a better chance of being forewarned. Fighters were deployed to protect both naval and air bases, with radar stations to alert them of incoming attacks.

As most German bases were well inside some of the long fjords there was also time for land spotters to play a role. Anti aircraft fire was increased dramatically as time went by and bases were protected with smoke dischargers to obscure them. Hence the big ships could lay at anchor with a certain level of security while they waited for the call to intercept a convoy.

German heavy units were always fearful of suffering damage that may result in them being intercepted and sunk by the British Home fleet. Hitler demanded his fleet achieve victories, but was also its biggest hindrance by also insisting that the big ships didn't take risks. Lack of sea time is bad for any fleet and the German battle fleet was severely restricted by fuel problems. Without sea time units cannot train and without training they lack the efficiency required by wartime operations.

Thus the German naval forces had some considerable advantages of comfort over their allied opponents, even if such things often meant a lower standard of combat experience and the efficiency that comes with sea time. As a result of the lack of training, and mad directives from Hitler, the fleet failed in most of its operations, showing a lack of tactical skill. It also showed the Admirals unwilling to fight, lest they be held to blame by the Fuhrer for ships lost and damaged. Such is not a good environment for successful operations.

The British were not fully aware of this and had to always expect the German fleet would do something

## THE BRITISH SITUATION

The British Royal Navy was already stretched to breaking point when Russia entered the war. It had international responsibilities to uphold all over the world, many battles to fight, and rising high above all these was the need to keep the United Kingdom itself supplied. Food and war material was available, but these had to be got in to the ports that waited for it. The Germans were putting the pressure on them in the North Atlantic in particular and the need to escort so many convoys was a huge drain on a navy reeling from heavy losses.

Therefore when Winston Churchill told the Admiralty that the British Government was committed to the supply of materials to Russia there was considerable dismay. The Western Approaches Command was already struggling to defeat the U Boat menace. It could spare little for a new front. However, Churchill made it known that he expected the Admiralty to find a way, even if it meant committing major units of the Home Fleet to the task.

This was not to suppose that the Home Fleet itself was bulging with resources. It had suffered serious losses in earlier operations. Many of its units had been sent to distant combat zones to hold back the tide of Axis advances that could threaten the very sources of supply the British relied upon. Many new ships were on the way and as they joined some could be diverted. But part of the problem lay in the very location of the only Soviet ports that could be supplied.

Having agreed to send the supplies demanded by Stalin, into northern ports, Churchill left it to his Admirals to decide how. A British mission to Murmansk found the port was woefully inadequate to handle large amounts of material. The wharf areas were limited, warehouses lacking and such basic things as cranes for unloading, were almost completely absent. This meant that the facilities would have to be provided, in addition to running the supplies.

## THE CONVOYS

For the Allies the strategic situation was a difficult one. A force of ships had to be gathered together for each convoy, because they did not run as often as those across the Atlantic and other places. To have valuable warships sitting around doing nothing was a luxury the British could not afford.

The Home Fleet was given the task of running convoys to Russia as the Western Approaches command had more than enough to do in its own area of operations. Via Admiralty intervention some escorts were borrowed from that command if the situation permitted. Ships newly commissioned or fresh from refit were also drawn in for close escort duties. Others were borrowed from the UK East Coast convoy area. The units allocated were efficient enough, but unlike the Atlantic escort groups, were often not as familiar in operations together. When a permanent escort group was borrowed, it usually performed well, but this could not always be done.

A convoy assembled in Scotland would usually be accompanied by a force known as the local escort. This comprised mostly old destroyers with a short range. It may also include a minesweeper or two, or warships on passage to the USA for refit that were added to the screen to make their journey more useful.

With the convoy from the start, there would usually be some escorts that would continue all the way to journey's end. These would be types such as destroyers converted to long range escorts, sloops, frigates and corvettes. If an escort carrier was to be present it would usually sail with the convoy from the start. The carrier carried enough fuel to feed hungry escorts. Therefore an old destroyer might be allocated to it as a plane guard to rescue downed pilots and provide personal escort should the carrier has to operate detached.

The fighting escort of a convoy had to come from the Home Fleet itself and would mostly comprise destroyers of the latest types. Such ships are designed for a role in fleet actions and although well practiced at this, post war analysis shows that they were much less efficient at ASW duties. A destroyer is also a thirsty ship when engaged in the back and forth work around a convoy, with a need to refuel more often than the plodding corvettes or sloops.

The United States of America had vast resources and made enormous amounts of war material available to the USSR as soon as possible. But the US Navy was embroiled in a deadly naval struggle in the Pacific, for which it needed the bulk of its fleet. On occasion the US Navy sent some large units to help the RN with the task of confining the German northern fleet. It was noted by British observers that these ships generally fared better than their own warships, being more comfortable and better designed for cold conditions.

Near the latitude of Iceland there would be a rendezvous point. Here the short range escorts of the local group would detach, proceed to Seidisfjord in Iceland to refuel, and wait for a convoy going back to the UK. They would be replaced by others that had been positioned in Seidisfjord or Reykjavik in advance, which would enable them to join the convoy fresh from being refueled and provisioned by the Royal Fleet Auxiliaries stationed in Iceland for that purpose.

The newly arrived escorts would take up position. Some might be allocated to the close escort. Generally most of this group would comprise what was known as the fighting escort. These ships were usually powerful destroyers of recent construction, detached from the Home Fleet for the job. They may or may not have a cruiser with them.

Having set out from Scotland, then reshuffled escorts off Iceland, the convoy would proceed to Russia. The position of the pack ice line determined how much distance could be kept between them and Norway. In winter it came down around Jan Mayen and Bear Island, forcing the convoy to keep much further south than in summer.

In winter the convoy would be run mostly in darkness, with only brief periods of twilight because the sun did not rise over the horizon by day. Massive storms would make passage difficult but in between the intense cold caused problems of its own. Ships tended to ice up. That is to say, that as spray came over the bows it turned to ice, which then adhered to every possible holding. Even the rigging became festooned with ice. Guns became inoperable, decks impassable, and life was miserable. The ice could be chipped off, or reduced with steam hoses, but it was a difficult job that was not always possible in some weather conditions. None the less it was vital. A ship with many tons of ice up top becomes unstable and in danger of capsize. It has to be got rid of as often as possible, placing an arduous burden on the crew members.

As assembled the convoy would have a forward and outer screen that was the place of the fighting escort. Around the convoy it would be the close escort. If a carrier was present it would have a couple of spaces left vacant for it within the columns of merchant ships. This gave it room for maneuver when operating aircraft. If a cruiser or an auxiliary AA ship was present, positions would be allocated within the convoy from which their guns could provide covering fire.

An important element near the rear would be one or usually two, tankers. These carried bunker fuel so that escorts in need of fuel could obtain it. Unfortunately the RN was not very advanced in this technique of refueling at sea, during WW2. Hence the weather needed to be fairly calm for it to take place. The tankers were not as advanced as those of the USN and incapable of alongside refueling. Instead fuel hoses were trailed over the stern and ships using them had to follow along behind at the same speed as the tanker.

Vital to the safety of all were the rescue ships. Many were small merchant ships fitted with medical facilities and extra berths. They were not hospital ships and ineligible for protection under the Red Cross. Therefore they were well armed for their size. Most also carried HF/DF equipment to help locate U Boat signals. If a special rescue ship was not available the task was usually allocated to a naval trawler or two. Apart from these it was not normal practice for the other ships to rescue survivors of other ships. It was done. Many captains were not prepared to leave seamen to die in the frozen waters, and would make the effort. But in general it was not encouraged as the ship itself could make itself a target. Warships might also take off survivors or pick them up, where possible, but this was always very much secondary to their role of ensuring the safety of the other ships in their charge.

## THE WINTER PASSAGE

Occasional icebergs were present, but radar reduced the danger of these. What was difficult to avoid was floating ice known as grumblers. These were sections of relatively flat ice, which had broken free from the pack ice line. While smaller than icebergs, they were quite capable of inflicting damage, and much harder to see. Entering a floating icepack meant the convoy would have to slow down and ships would have to take great care to avoid damage. The presence of an icebreaker would be irrelevant as the ice was already broken up. It was not uncommon for warships to suffer damage to their ASW search domes in such conditions.

When icing took place, it could also affect such things as radar aerials. If these froze in place, their use was limited. If they froze up entirely they just did not work. In some cases, they might give false echoes from floating ice, from sleet, or other dense storm activity. Radar was of extreme value but could not always be relied upon to work.

Icing up also occurred in extreme cold conditions, when a warship was required to increase speed. Battleships and cruisers would be less affected as they had more freeboard, but destroyers in particular could find it difficult to keep up with the large ships they were escorting, if speed was called for.

Fog could be both a help and a hindrance. Ships carried fog buoys that they could stream behind them. They carried a dull blue light that a following ship could see in order to avoid a collision. Never the less hips still did collided from time to time.

If high enough fog could be a friend and hide the convoy from sight. But on other occasions while the ships were struggling to see each other, their mast tops would be visible above the fog bank, inviting attacks from aircraft they could not see.

A dark Arctic night offered concealment. But it was not always so. In those waters the brilliant lights of the Aurora could light up the convoy more brightly than the murky twilight of what passed for daytime. In such a situation the ships would be easy for a U Boat to see and to attack. An Aurora was also an opportunity for the Luftwaffe to launch night attacks, using the brightness of these northern lights as a convenient illumination. Darkness was thus not always a friend.

Air attacks were less common during winter convoy operations. But the Luftwaffe was quite skilled at using an aircraft to drop flares to mark targets they had located with airborne radar. Such tactics could be used during the dull days of poor twilight, when there was sufficient light for the attackers to fly low and be able to see the ocean. It could be used in total darkness, but that was much more difficult as a less skilled crew could become disoriented and crash.

For this reason air attacks were far less frequent in winter. They were also no doubt affected by the extreme weather conditions experienced by the northern bases of the Luftwaffe. To compensate, winter with its long hours of darkness was the time when heavy units of the Kriegsmarine put to sea. Long hours of darkness provided concealment for a fleet that was always heavily outnumbered.

Such cold conditions sometimes produced strange effects. For example, the discharge from the diesel engines of a U Boat could form a dense column when it operated on the surface, making it visible for miles.

In Arctic waters, there could be several layers of thermocline. This could make search conditions very difficult, as U Boats would hide under them. But at the same time these conditions could degrade the hydrophones of U Boats to such a level that they would need to come above the layers to hear what was going on. On other occasions, the water could be so clear that ASW searches were enhanced.

## THE SUMMER PASSAGE

During the short summer months the ice pack retreated almost to Greenland, Spitsbergen and Novaya Zemlya. Because of the need to pass so close to German airfields there was a need for air cover, which was provided occasionally by fleet carriers that operated with the main fleet. As time went on smaller escort carriers were provided and while some of the American built ones served on the runs to Russia, much of the effort was borne by the handful of British built ships.

At first the British and then the Americans had to send fighters to the Murman coast to provide some measure of air cover. This role was gradually taken over by the Soviets, often flying the aircraft delivered by convoys. Eventually Russian air cover improved, but in the early period of convoys the pressure on other fronts precluded the USSR from deploying enough aircraft to the north. Allied pilots who operated from the region had mixed experiences, with some reporting their red allies friendly and others that they were always uncooperative and obstructionist.

By the height of the German attacks on convoys to Russia, Allied anti submarine tactics were well developed. Improved weapons were also starting to appear. The number of escorts available was not only on the increase, but in addition they were of improved types which were now pouring out of the shipyards. In addition most warships were fitted with radar which in combination with all the other factors forced the U Boats to adopt different means of attack.

In earlier operations against Atlantic convoys the U Boats could wait until night, and then dash in to attack. This was particularly effective when several boats formed a wolf pack. At night they were very hard to see and much success was achieved. However radar could reduce the effect of such attacks by allowing the ASW escorts to see surfaced submarines despite the darkness.

In the northern summer U Boats found very little darkness to hide in as there could be days of almost perpetual daylight. Additionally most escorts had radar. To attack on the surface by day was suicidal, therefore in summer most attacks had to be carried out from safe, submerged positions. Such positions were of course hard to achieve because not only were the escorts well equipped and numerous, they were often arranged in outer and inner screens. This meant a U Boat would have to penetrate deeper defenses that were covered by better equipped escorts.

Almost complete daylight also meant German surface ships could only operate in a situation of extreme risk. Despite having some powerful ships, the reality was that the British navy was far more numerous. Aircraft carriers were of great danger should they catch German warships at sea. Not only could they provide advance warning of an attack, they also had the ability to strike long before a task force could reach the convoys. Considering the number of ships deployed by the Home Fleet, it was probable that any Kriegsmarine ships that were damaged and slowed down could be caught and destroyed. The value of the threat of German heavy ships would not be worth anything if the vessels were sunk or severely damaged. This meant that the eternal days of summer were too dangerous for surface operations.

Despite the problems, the Kriegsmarine were committed to try to stop the constant flow of war material to the Eastern Front. Its submarine force was prepared to make attacks and accept losses in order to support their comrades struggling against the Soviet Army. But it still needed help in pinning down where the convoys were and such help would have to come from the Luftwaffe.

There were numerous requests from the German navy, for the Luftwaffe to make a greater effort against the Russian convoys. Most were received positively enough by German Supreme HQ and Reichmarschall Goering was instructed by Hitler to deploy his forces accordingly. However all German operations were subject to jealousy between the armed forces.

Goering was reluctant to do anything that could be seen as subordinate to the navy. He resisted early advice to train aircrews for torpedo attack and continually put the value of anti shipping attacks on the bottom of his list of priorities. Eventually he was forced to commit aircraft to torpedo bombing and to put more effort into shipping attacks. The results were sometimes below average, but often were much more successful than expected. It was the successes that persuaded Goering that attacking the summer convoys could be worthwhile. But with rivalry still in mind these plans often failed to take into account anything the navy was doing, or to cooperate with submarine attacks.

Because of this, German operations against summer convoys to Russia were rarely coordinated. The Luftwaffe went about its business and the Kriegsmarine its own. Pleas for air reconnaissance were met with insufficient response unless the Luftwaffe itself was prepared to located convoys it could attack. The glory was seen in sinking's. Damaging ships for submarines to finish off later was not seen to be of as much value in the competitive atmosphere of the High Command back in Berlin.

Air tactics put into use included the notorious and very deadly Golden Zange. This was carried out by a large number of aircraft flying in a single wing tip to wing tip line. Types used were usually He111's or Ju88's and they carried either one or two torpedoes.

The formation could approach from a slight angle to the convoy lines, or dead abeam. On reaching about 1,500yds from the convoy lines each aircraft dropped a torpedo. At 1,000yds it banked slightly and dropped the second, after which it was free to evade the AA fire, which was usually quite heavy.

For the convoy the attack presented a dilemma because the number of incoming torpedoes was rather more than most ships lookouts could cope with. They would be coming in two waves and two angles. Evading one could put a ship in peril from another. Even having the entire convoy turn into an attack would not necessarily work as the second wave would be approaching on another bearing. Then there was the difficulty that ships one or two row in, may have their view blocked by outer ships. To this was added the peril presented by ships breaking formation to evade, which in itself made the danger of collision higher.

On occasion a U Boat might find itself in position to add to the confusion and distract escorts. Stragglers and damaged ships that became detached from the convoy could be picked off by nearby submarines. In addition other aircraft equipped with bombs were ready to pounce on them.

Fortunately for the Convoys, the Luftwaffe did not always have sufficient strength for such an intense attack. Aircraft provided were varied and the training of the crews equally varied. As a result the type of attacks could vary from high level bombing, through to medium and low level, as well as dive bombing. The warship screen had to be on its toes for all kinds of air assault On many occasions the presence of a single scout aircraft was enough to guide in an attack. Therefore, having the advantage of operating at relatively short ranges, the attackers could fly in at low level, remaining below radar cover. The need to conserve fuel was not a limitation when working so close to its own bases. This meant the ability to remain low and avoid detection, even if they later had to climb for their actual attack.

The allies tried to drive off the various reconnaissance aircraft through providing escort carriers or CAM ships. This was often effective. But the speed margin between some of the German aircraft types used, and the fighters employed by the convoy were not great. By the time a fighter had climbed high enough to intercept, many scouts could be far enough away to avoid being attacked. The provision of a combat air patrol (CAP) did help and as reconnaissance aircraft flew high, early radar detection could keep them at bay. But even this was not a guarantee. Aircraft being driven off from a particular area, but not others, indicates that the convoy must be in the black zone created.

Having sufficient aircraft up to intercept attacks was problematic. German aircraft operating from land bases might well be able to get into the air in conditions more favorable than those over the convoy itself. At sea the escort carriers could be struggling through in conditions too rough for them to launch. One could not presume that just because the
weather was bad over the convoy, that an air attack from land bases was unlikely.

In summer the Soviets preferred the Allies to push on to Arkangelsk, rather than Murmansk. It had good practical reasons as the supplies were then delivered to a port more capable of handling them and free of the constant attacks the closer port had to endure. But Arkangelsk also meant more days at sea for the Allies, and therefore more opportunities for the Germans to attack. It is true that as they moved closer to Arkangelsk the range from Luftwaffe bases lengthened. But the danger from submarines and mines actually increased.

## The Luftwaffe in the Arctic

Reichmarschall Goering was head of the Luftwaffe but was always keen to ensure his forces gained the Lions share of praise for victories. Thus like most of the other Nazi forces, there was considerable jealousy and a lack of cooperation. During the early convoys to Russia he was told by Hitler to assist the Kriegsmarine in its operations. However just as in the Atlantic, the help supplied was limited, given tardily and often unhelpful. Aircraft sent to Northern Norway were second line and certainly not the best crews. Results were therefore poor and actual help given to the navy very limited.

With the struggle in Russia growing more and more deadly, Hitler urged Goering to make a greater effort to help stop allied convoys delivering ammunition, aircraft, tanks and other war supplies to the Arctic ports. His response was to send attack groups so the Luftwaffe could gain glory by stopping the convoys, rather than making a serious attempt to work with the German Navy. Reconnaissance was improved, but all too often the intelligence passed on was lacking detail and accuracy.

Instead at various points the Luftwaffe launched heavy air attacks that were not coordinated with the Kriegsmarine. These were damaging and for a time caused the Allies to suspend convoys during summer. But this required crack units and such were in high demand on other fronts. As a result the air units available fluctuated up and down according to the need of other fronts.

A problem faced by the Luftwaffe was one that had been seen early by the Kriegsmarine, but which Goering had failed to address. This was the difficulty of navigation over water for long distances. There were only a few groups trained for this task and all these were engaged on reconnaissance duty. Thus although air attacks were feasible for much of the distance the convoys had to travel, the strongest attacks had to be reserved for when the ships had to pass close to air bases in northern Norway. Here intensive air strikes could be carried out and sometimes with several per day. They were damaging and they sank many ships, but the failure to subject the convoys to heavy air attack for much more of their passage was an opportunity lost. It certainly contrasted with Allied operations over the sea and particularly operations by both sides in the Pacific.

There was another problem unique to the region. In most areas if an aircrew were shot down they at least had some chance to bail out and parachute to safety, or they could attempt to crash land and escape. But over Arctic waters to be shot down was a sure death sentence. Survival time of a man in the freezing waters could be as little as three minutes. Even in a raft the survivors would face death from wind chill and the extreme cold. Pilots are generally mindful of the welfare of their crew members, who after all are their companions in danger. Because of this it was found that pilots who were totally carefree and reckless in other regions, were very cautious over Arctic waters. There was a reluctance to get in too close if the flak was heavy because even if not shot down, any damage that forced the aircraft to ditch on the way home was bound to be fatal for the crew. Luftwaffe crews still showed great skill and some did take amazing risks, but in general skill predominated over risk. Hence many torpedo attacks were launched with great thought, but from longer ranges than in the Mediterranean for example.

Luftwaffe aircraft that did work with the Kriegsmarine on reconnaissance duty were usually manned by good crews and were much more confident about flying for long distances over the seas. Poor communication with the Navy spoilt many of their efforts as signals had to pass through the correct chain of command, rather than direct. Navigational errors were certainly not exclusive to them, as the Allies had similar problems with aircraft over the ocean, but such errors did often make it hard to relocate convoys they reported.

By the time the biggest convoys were sailing for Russia the Luftwaffe had radar equipped aircraft in the region and this made searching much easier. It also allowed them to remain further away, which was very important with the Allies adding escort carriers to the protective forces of convoys. Radar gave them a greater chance of evading fighters and surviving, once again a matter of great importance to the crew when flying over such inhospitable waters.

Russia's summer port at Murmansk was within short flying range of Luftwaffe bases for most of WW2. So even having reached Kola ships still had to negotiate the entrance to Murmansk under air attack and the threat of mines laid by aircraft and which were continually replenished. Ships that had struggled through all kinds of difficulties to reach Murmansk could find themselves being bombed and sunk while waiting to unload or while alongside the wharf discharging their cargo. The Soviets increased the anti aircraft strength of the area at a steady rate until the amount of flak put up from Murmansk was very heavy indeed. But that could not stop the aerial minelaying efforts further away, nor prevent strikes against shipping while arriving or leaving.

The situation for the port of Archangelsk was far better but it was only open during summer. The port was still within air attack range, but much further away and with considerable fighter defences covering the route. Because of this the Luftwaffe contented itself with a very intense aerial minelaying program that failed to close the Gourlo, which is the entry route to the White Sea. None the less the mining effort did inflict many casualties on Allied shipping and cause them to deploy many minesweepers to counter the program.

### SIGHTINGS AND BEARINGS

RED = Port. (Left)
GREEN = Starboard. (Right)
Bearings to a sighting were frequently given as red or green, followed by a degree from the bow of the ship.
For example 'Ship bearing RED 90 Range 3 miles'. This would indicate that there was a ship at 3 miles range on the port side and ninety degrees from the bow of the sighting ship.
'Aircraft GREEN 30, low two miles'. Would indicate an aircraft 30 degrees from the starboard bow, low down and are two miles distant.

The sequence told all other lookouts and officers firstly what to look for, which side of the ship, what angle of bearing, and lastly how far away. If the lookout was able to do so he would also add more detail such as if the sighting was unknown, an enemy, or friendly.

**In this game all sightings will be given using the above system.**

## SO HOW DO WE START PLAYING?

Firstly follow the steps to determine which year and route you will be using. Then follow through with selection of ships to be convoyed and the escort available to them.

## HANDLING A CONVOY ON THE PLAYING AREA

Convoys are laid out on a tabletop in the columns and lines shown in the appropriate diagrams. Not all columns or line positions have to be filled. It was normal practice to make a convoy wider than it was deep, to avoid long flanks that would be easier for the enemy to attack. Therefore a small convoy of only eight ships could well have only four columns, each of two ships. A Nine ship convoy may use five columns, but with a single ship in one column.

Escorts are placed according to the alphabetical positions shown. It is unlikely you will have sufficient escorts to fill every position, but it makes it easier for you if you keep track of them according to the position they are filling, when contacts are reported to you.

During the game, the convoy merchant ships are not moved. They are placed in their columns and lines, but to make the game move fast they are left in those positions unless damage or other events cause them to fall out of position. The escorts similarly do not move unless something occurs that causes them to act independently. This makes the game much faster as there is no need to move every ship, every move. With a large convoy this would be an arduous and time-consuming business. Instead, everything that happens around the convoy is moved relative to it. Rather like a satellite around a planet. The convoy is always placed in the centre of the playing area.

After years of practice I have found it convenient to place the merchant ships on a board the size of a convoy, and distribute the escort ships around it. If a radical change of course takes place it is then possible to simply turn the whole board to the new course without having to move every single ship. This is the culmination of almost 30 years of fighting convoy wargames and it is by far the quickest way. Some of my boards are clear plastic, so the normal naval tabletop can be seen through them. I also have some painted for special sea conditions, such as one for the Arctic.

When non-convoy vessels or U Boats appear, they will be declared as in a specific position. When players move them, they carry out their normal move first, and then they move the models 'relative to the course of the convoy'. Therefore is coming in from one edge, a U Boat might move 15 knots on the surface in the normal manner, but then depending on the speed of the convoy, it will be moved as if it was the convoy that was moving. This can prove a tricky navigation problem for the unwary, as you not only calculate where you want to move, but where your vessel will end up, relative to the direction and speed of the convoy. For example, you come in at right angles from the edge of the table at 15 knots, and do a move as normal. But then because the convoy is moving at 11 knots, you will have to move eleven knots directly down the table toward the rear of the convoy, as if it was steaming past. Of course this means you have to be very careful when entering the lines of a convoy. It is easy to make a mistake and find out that you have collided with, or been run down by, one of the merchant ships.

Similarly once the escorts start moving independently, they too do a normal type move, but then are moved down the playing area at the speed of the convoy.

## HOW THE GAME RUNS

**Once you have selected your convoy**, its route and its escorts, proceed to the map.

**Coloured event boxes** equate to which convoy you are running. The boxes each represent a time period. The number inside each coloured box indicates which event box to roll on for that campaign move. Some boxes are shaded, representing a night move. Arrival and departure zones are also shown. Commence at the departure point with a die roll for the area indicated. The convoy then progresses along its route rolling for results on the appropriate boxes. Contacts are fought out before moving on to the next event box.

**Event boxes** Day, night, etc. There are many chance factors and some of these create others, therefore no two convoys should experience the same passage, even though some events might be the same or similar on different days or nights. In play testing some convoys have run through with very little action. The majority have a pretty busy time of it, and an occasional convoy will have a nightmare run, with contact after contact that will test the skill of the players for it to even survive at all.

**Runners and Investigation boxes** As a result of various things that happen, you will from time to time, be referred to some boxes that give unknown contacts and so forth. These just enter the game in sequence with the event boxes and are easy to understand.

**Surfaced submarines** This occurs a lot during night moves. In play testing it was found best to put them on the playing area and move them in the normal manner. Until detected visually or by radar, no ship can act against them and they must therefore proceed as if the presence of the U Boat was unknown. If detected, escorts can act, but it is important to roll for each escort that is in a position to detect. Some may fail to do so even though others have. If the detecting boat illuminates the U Boat, then others within visual may engage it if they are in range.

**Combat** between the convoy, aircraft, U-boats or surface ships, is carried out using the combat resolution rule tables.

**Torpedoes** In the majority of cases the torpedo will reach its target in a single move, and if not sighted there will be no evasive action. Therefore players can simply proceed straight to determination of hits, and damage resolution. At night torpedo tracks were not visible. By day tracks of the G3e torpedo were also not visible.

**Close defence** In this y period, Allied policy was close defence of the convoy by the through escort, but the attached escorts and fighting screen could be detached to hut U Boat contacts to destruction. As will be seen from tactical charts in this volume, the convoys adopted a two ring defence against submarine attack. Against air attack they would adopt a different formation which is again shown. If there was a threat of contact with enemy surface vessels yet other formations could be adopted.

**Game referees** may choose to control some contacts until their identity is established.

**ALLIED PLAYERS** are expected to control the convoy and escorts under their command. Their contribution to the game, and the mini campaign, is their skill in the tactical direction of defending their charges. The commanders at sea had no idea of 'the big picture'. That was the province of the Admiralty. While in command of your convoy you will receive a certain amount of information. But apart from that you will be as in the dark as the real life commanders were but still required to meet everything the enemy throw at you.

## HOW TO ESTABLISH THE SIZE OF A CONVOY

Convoys sailed in columns. Usually a convoy was much wider than deep. Up to ten columns wide on the Arctic run, but probably only three or four ships deep. At times they had to reduce this to one or two columns to pass through a minefield or negotiated a channel cleared through the ice for them.

Recognizing that now all wargamers will have the same merchant ships available, and even if of the same types, players will probably have assigned different names, the 'convoy calculator' can be used. This also allows the game organizer to know what ships to have out and damage charts ready. Being able to do this will cut down preparation time considerable when the players are ready to start a game.

Firstly fill in each column and row with the names of the ship models you have available. Provision is made for twelve columns, each of three ships. Convoys to and from Gibraltar were rarely as large as those that crossed the Atlantic.

The chart will generate convoys of a size to be reasonably expected. These will vary between 36 and 14 merchant ships. In some cases one may be a rescue ship or a CAM ship. However these were merchant manned and are therefore part of the merchant ship total. The rescue ship does not carry cargo, but a CAM ship does.

Roll a d10 and consult the composition table. That shows which columns and rows to remove. The ships that remain form your convoy.

Note that they are deliberately removed in such a manner as not to upset the numbering of columns and rows.

The chart shows how many columns, ships, speed and route to be followed.

## NATIONALITIES

When filling in the convoy names, remember that Allied convoys were made up of ships from a whole range of nationalities. The most common for ARCTIC STORM would be British, Norwegian, American, Dutch and Polish. But others could be found in convoys of this type as well.

## THE ESCORT GENERATOR

Fill in the columns with the model ships you have available. If these are limited in number you can use the same ship in several columns as it won't be chosen twice.

Note the designation SOE. This indicates which ship will be the flagship of the Senior Officer Escorts.

Some rows indicate a specific ship type. Anti Aircraft ships may also be included. ASW Trawlers are a compulsory part of the escort group if shown and were often vital in performing rescue duties to save crews that would otherwise have been left to die in the freezing waters.

Roll a D10 and consult the chart. The column rolled becomes the escort for your convoy.
The escort for a convoy can therefore vary in number and type. It is permissible to also have a CAM ship as part of the merchant vessels.

## LOCAL ESCORT GENERATOR

Once having selected the convoy and its escort follow the same procedure for any local escort available from the port of departure. In this instance the types of ship you should use are indicated.

They will usually be ships of older types, short ranged, or simply detached temporarily from other duties.

Because they have other duties these local escorts will have to turn back at a given time, regardless of the situation of the convoy. However with convoys to Russia they will usually be replaced by other ships.

When the convoys near Russian ports there will be occasions when escorts from those areas will join for the last leg of the route. Most of these will be Soviet ships, whose AA contributions were always welcome. They were however very indifferent anti submarine ships and not well equipped for that role. There were also some British pre war sloops of the Halcyon class stationed in north Russia at Soviet request. These ships were mainly intended as minesweepers but proved to be excellent sea boats in Arctic conditions and efficient ASW escorts as well. Toward the end of the war the newer Algerine type were also sent north, but the enormous contribution of the Halcyon class vessels should not be overlooked. In the later period the Soviets also received various ships from the Allies. These were fitted with up to date equipment and enabled the Soviets to provide better support for their own and Allied convoys.

## DECIDING THE COMPOSITION OF A CONVOY

### Convoy Calculator

| COLUMN 1 | COLUMN 2 | COLUMN 3 | COLUMN 4 | COLUMN 5 | COLUMN 6 | COLUMN 7 | COLUMN 8 | COLUMN 9 | COLUMN 10 |
|---|---|---|---|---|---|---|---|---|---|
| 1 AK | 21 AK | 31 AO | 41 AK | 51 AK | 61 AK | 71 AO | 81 AK | 91 AK | 101 AK |
| 12 AK | 22 AO | 32 AE | 42 AE | 52 AO | 62 AO | 72 AE | 82 AK | 92 AK | 102 AK |
| 13 AK | 23 AK | 33 AC | 43 AK | 53 AK | 63 Rescue ship | 73 AK | 83 | 93 AK | 103 AK |
| 14 | 24 | 34 | 44 | 54 CAM SHIP | 64 | 74 | 84 | 94 | 104 |
| 15 | 25 | 35 | 45 | 55 | 65 | 75 | 85 CAM SHIP | 95 | 105 |

### COMPOSITION OF A CONVOY

| D10 | Alterations | Columns | ships | Speed | | PERIOD | Destination. |
|---|---|---|---|---|---|---|---|
| 1 | Convoy composition remains as shown | 10 of 5 | 50 | Slow | 7knots | WINTER | Scotland to Murmansk |
| 2 | Remove row 5 | 10 of 4 | 40 | Slow | 7knots | SUMMER | Scotland to Arkangelsk |
| 3 | Remove row 5 and column 10 | 9 of 4 | 36 | Slow | 7knots | WINTER | Scotland to Murmansk |
| 4 | Remove rows 5 and 4 | 10 of 3 | 30 | Slow | 7knots | WINTER | Scotland to Murmansk |
| 5 | Remove rows 5 & 4 plus column &10 | 9 of 3 | 27 | Slow | 7knots | WINTER | Scotland to Murmansk |
| 6 | Remove row 5 &4 plus columns 9 &10 | 8 of 3 | 24 | Slow | 7knots | WINTER | Scotland to Murmansk |
| 7 | Remove row 4 & 5 column 8, 9 & 10 | 7 of 3 | 21 | Slow | 7knots | SUMMER | Scotland to Arkangelsk |
| 8 | Remove row 4 & 5 column 8, 9 & 10 | 7 of 3 | 18 | Slow | 7knots | WINTER | Scotland to Murmansk |
| 9 | Remove row 3, 4 & 5 column 9 & 10 | 8 of 2 | 16 | Slow | 7knots | SUMMER | Scotland to Arkangelsk |
| 0 | Remove row 3, 4 & 5 column 8, 9 & 10 | 7 of 2 | 14 | Slow | 7knots | SUMMER | Scotland to Arkangelsk |
| 1-2 | Pre set size | 1 of 2 | 3 | Slow | 7knots | SUMMER | Lagerni to Arkangelsk |
| 3-4 | Pre set size | 2 of 2 | 4 | Slow | 7knots | SUMMER | Lagerni to Murmansk |
| 5-6 | Pre set size | 2 of 3 | 6 | Slow | 7knots | SUMMER | Karmaluky to Kara Strait |
| 7-8 | Pre set size | 2 of 3 | 6 | Slow | 7knots | SUMMER | Kara strain to Murmansk |
| 9-0 | Pre set size | 2 of 2 | 4 | Slow | 7knots | SUMMER | Kara strait to Archangelsk |

Allied Convoys to Russia often had to endure low visibility and some areas of restricted passage, especially when they encountered ice. Radar was also now more available. Therefore they were often not as wide as Allied convoys in other areas and sometimes had more ships to a column.

Soviet convoys were only run during summer and were always very small. They mostly ran supplies to remote outposts. Return convoys carried furs, frozen fish, tinned fish and mined ore. A vital commodity was fish oil which was used in the making of explosives. Summer was also the only time the northern route across the top of the world, could be used. This enabled warships to be transferred from the Pacific fleet as well as various cargoes. The route was not open every summer but during WW2 was used on several occasions. The need to pass through narrow areas or gaps in minefields meant the convoys were never more than two ships wide and often had to move in single file.

## LOCAL UK ESCORT GENERATOR 1942

| Escort Group 1-4 | Escort Group 5-6 | Escort Group 7-8 | Escort Group 9-0 |
|---|---|---|---|
| Old S DD | V&W SRE | V&W | WAIR |
| Hunt 1 | Old S DD | Old S DD | SRE |
| Flower | Old R DD | Old S DD | SRE |
| Bangor | Hunt 1 | Flower | Old S DD |
| Bangor | Kingfisher | Flower | Hunt I |

With convoy from Scotland these ships detach when the convoy reaches waters off Iceland and proceed to Iceland to refuel before joining a convoy bound for The UK

## THROUGH ESCORT GENERATOR 1942

| Escort Group 1-4 | Escort Group 5-6 | Escort Group 7-8 | Escort Group 9-0 |
|---|---|---|---|
| Blackswan | Blackswan | Blackswan | I class DD |
| Grimsby | V&W LRE | Bittern | Hunt II |
| Halcyon | Flower | Shoreham | Hunt II |
| Halcyon | Flower | Flower | Blackswan |
| Flower | Flower | Flower | Halcyon |
| Aux AA | Flower | Flower | Halcyon |
| Trawler | Flower | Aux AA | Flower |
| Trawler | Trawler | Trawler | Flower |

Escort groups in red are from Western Approaches with special ASW tactics training

Escort with convoy from Scotland through to Russia

## ICELANDIC ESCORT GENERATOR 1942

| Escort Group 1-4 | Escort Group 5-6 | Escort Group 7-8 | Escort Group 9-0 |
|---|---|---|---|
| Grimsby | Hunt II | Hunt III | Hunt II |
| Shoreham | Grimsby | Hunt II | Hunt II |
| Flower | Flower | Town DD | Flower |
| Flower | Flower | Grimsby | Flower |
|  | Trawler | Flower | Halcyon |
|  |  | Flower | Trawler |

These escorts join convoy from Iceland with merchant ships From that port and then become part of the through escort Under the command of the SOE

## FIGHTING ESCORT GENERATOR 1942

| Fighting Escort 1-3 | Fighting Escort 4-5 | Fighting Escort 6-7 | Fighting Escort 8-9 | Fighting Escort 0 |
|---|---|---|---|---|
| Dido CL | Dido CL | County CA | Southampton | County CA |
| Tribal DD | Tribal DD | Colony CL | Colony CL | Southampton |
| O class DD | I class DD | Tribal DD | Tribal DD | M class DD |
| O class DD | O class DD | O class DD | M class DD | M class DD |
|  | O class DD | O class DD | Q class DD | M class DD |
|  |  | Q class DD | O class DD | O class DD |
|  |  |  | O class DD | Q class DD |

Join the convoy from Seidisfjord as force to engage if Enemy surface forces attack the convoy and as extra AA and ASW protection

## LOCAL UK ESCORT GENERATOR 1943

| Escort Group 1-4 | Escort Group 5-6 | Escort Group 7-8 | Escort Group 9-0 |
|---|---|---|---|
| SRE | SRE | Wallace | Scott DD |
| Old S DD | SRE | Town DD | WAIR |
| Hunt 1 | Old S DD | Town DD | Hunt II |
| Hunt 1 | Old R DD | Hunt I | Hunt III |
| Kingfisher | Hunt III | Hunt IV |  |

With convoy from Scotland these ships detach when the convoy reaches waters off Iceland and proceed to Seidisfjord or Reykjavik to refuel and before joining a convoy bound for the UK

## THROUGH ESCORT GENERATOR 1943

| Escort Group 1-4 | Escort Group 5-6 | Escort Group 7-8 | Escort Group 9-0 |
|---|---|---|---|
| Blackswan | Biter CVE | Biter CVE | Archer CVE |
| Bittern | I class DD | Blackswan | A-I class DD |
| River | V&W LRE | Grimsby | A-I class DD |
| Flower | River | River | LRE |
| Flower | Flower | Flower | Blackswan |
| Flower | Flower | Flower | Hunt 2 |
| Aux AA | Flower | Aux AA | Flower |
| Trawler | Flower | Trawler | Flower |

Escort groups in red are from Western Approaches with special ASW tactics training

Escort with convoy from Scotland through to Russia

## ICELANDIC ESCORT GENERATOR 1943

| Escort Group 1-4 | Escort Group 5-6 | Escort Group 7-8 | Escort Group 9-0 |
|---|---|---|---|
| Grimsby | Hunt II | Hunt II | A-I DD |
| River | River | Hunt II | A-I DD |
| Flower | Flower | Flower | V&W LRE |
| Flower | Flower | Flower | River |
|  | Trawler | Flower |  |
|  |  | Flower |  |

These escorts join convoy from Iceland with merchant ships From that port and then become part of the through escort Under the command of the SOE

## FIGHTING ESCORT GENERATOR 1943

| Fighting Escort 1-2 | Fighting Escort 3-4 | Fighting Escort 5-6 | Fighting Escort 7-8 | Fighting Escort 9-0 |
|---|---|---|---|---|
| Tribal DD | Tribal DD | Dido CL | Belfast CL | London CA |
| O class DD | A-I DD | S class DD | Colony CL | Dido CL |
| O class DD | A-I DD | S class DD | M class DD | M class DD |
| O class DD | O class DD | O class DD | M class DD | S class DD |
|  | O class DD | O class DD | O class DD | S class DD |
|  |  |  | O class DD | O class DD |
|  |  |  | O class DD | O class DD |

Join the convoy from Seidisfjord as force to engage if Enemy surface forces attack the convoy and as extra AA and ASW protection

## LOCAL UK ESCORT GENERATOR 1944

| Escort Group 1-3 | Escort Group 4-6 | Escort Group 7-8 | Escort Group 9-0 |
|---|---|---|---|
| A-I DD | SRE | A-I DD | A-I DD |
| SRE | WAIR | River | A-I DD |
| Old S class | Hunt I | Crown Colony | Hunt II |
| Hunt I | Hunt II | Hunt II | Hunt II |
| Hunt I | Hunt III | Hunt II | Hunt II |
| Hunt I | Hunt IV | Hunt II | Hunt IV |

With convoy from Scotland these ships detach when the convoy reaches waters off Iceland and proceed to Seidisfjord or Reykjavik to refuel and before joining a convoy bound for the UK

## THROUGH ESCORT GENERATOR 1944

| Escort Group 1-4 | Escort Group 5-6 | Escort Group 7-8 | Escort Group 9-0 |
|---|---|---|---|
| Campania CVE | Activity CVE | Vindex CVE | Nairana CVE |
| Blackswan | I class DD | V&W LRE | V&W LRE |
| Loch | Loch | Captain DE | Captain DE |
| River | River | Captain DE | Loch |
| River | River | Blackswan | River |
| Castle | Flower | Loch | River |
| Flower | Flower | Crown Colony | Castle |
| Flower | Flower | Castle | Castle |

Escort groups in red are from Western Approaches with special ASW tactics training
Escort with convoy from Scotland through to Russia

## ICELANDIC ESCORT GENERATOR 1944

| Escort Group 5-8 | Escort Group 9-0 | Escort Group 4-7 | Escort Group 2 |
|---|---|---|---|
| River | River | A-I DD | A-I DD |
| River | River | A-I DD | V&W LRE |
| Flower | Flower | Hunt II | River |
| Flower | Flower | Hunt III | River |
| Flower | Flower | Algerine | Algerine |
| Algerine | Flower | Algerine | Algerine |

These escorts join convoy from Iceland with merchant ships
From that port and then become part of the through escort
Under the command of the SOE

## FIGHTING ESCORT GENERATOR 1944

| Fighting Escort 1-2 | Fighting Escort 3-4 | Fighting Escort 5-6 | Fighting Escort 7-8 | Fighting Escort 9-0 |
|---|---|---|---|---|
| Mod Dido CL | Dido CL | Colony | Colony | London CA |
| Tribal DD | Tribal DD | Dido CL | Mod Dido CL | Mod Dido CL |
| Tribal DD | A-I DD | S class DD | M class DD | V class DD |
| O class DD | A-I DD | S class DD | S class DD | V class DD |
| O class DD | O class DD | S class DD | V class DD | O class DD |
| O class DD | O class DD | S class DD | V class DD | O class DD |
| | | | V class DD | O class DD |

Join the convoy from Seidisfjord as force to engage if Enemy surface forces attack the convoy and as extra AA and ASW protection

## LOCAL UK ESCORT GENERATOR 1945

| Escort Group 5-8 | Escort Group 9-0 | Escort Group 1-3 | Escort Group 2 |
|---|---|---|---|
| A-I DD | Hunt III | Hunt II | I class DD |
| Catherine | Hunt IV | Hunt II | Hunt I |
| Catherine | Hunt II | Hunt II | Hunt II |
| Mod Flower | Hunt II | Mod. Flower | Hunt II |
| Flower | Hunt II | Flower | Hunt IV |
| Algerine | Algerine | Algerine | Algerine |
| Algerine | | | |

With convoy from Scotland these ships detach when the convoy reaches waters off Iceland and proceed to Seidisfjord or Reykjavik to refuel and before joining a convoy bound for the UK

## THROUGH ESCORT GENERATOR 1945

| Escort Group 1-4 | Escort Group 5-8 | Escort Group 9-0 | Escort Group 1-5 | Escort Group 6-0 |
|---|---|---|---|---|
| Battler CVE | Vindex CVE | Activity CVE | Campania CVE | Nairana CVE |
| Loch | Blackswan | Blackswan | Captain DE | Captain DE |
| River | Loch | Captain DE | Captain DE | Loch |
| River | River | River | Captain DE | Loch |
| Castle | Castle | River | Blackswan | River |
| Castle | Castle | Castle | Loch | River |
| Algerine | Flower | Flower | Crown Colony | Castle |
| Algerine | Flower | Flower | Crown Colony | Castle |

Units in red are Western Approaches units with special ASW tactics training
Escort with convoy from Scotland through to Russia

## ICELANDIC ESCORT GENERATOR 1945

| Escort Group 5-8 | Escort Group 9-0 | Escort Group 4-7 | Escort Group 2 |
|---|---|---|---|
| DD (Canada) | River | A-I DD | A-I DD |
| River(Canada) | River | A-I DD | Hunt II |
| River(Canada) | River | Hunt II | River |
| Flower(Canada) | Flower | Hunt III | River |
| Flower(Canada) | Flower | Flower | Algerine |
| Flower(Canada) | Flower | Flower | Algerine |

These escorts join convoy from Iceland with merchant ships
From that port and then become part of the through escort
Under the command of the SOE

## FIGHTING ESCORT GENERATOR 1945

| Fighting Escort 1-4 | Fighting Escort 5-8 | Fighting Escort 9-0 | Fighting Escort 1-3 | Fighting Escort 4-7 |
|---|---|---|---|---|
| Tribal DD | Battle DD | W class DD | Dido CL | Mod Dido CL |
| O class DD | Ca DD | W class DD | Ca class DD | Ca class DD |
| O class DD | Z class DD | W class DD | S class DD | Z class DD |
| O class DD | Z class DD | Z class DD | S class DD | Z class DD |
| | Z class DD | Z class DD | V class DD | S class DD |
| Units in red are Western Approaches units | | | Z class DD | S class DD |
| | | | Z class DD | S class DD |

Join the convoy from Seidisfjord as force to engage if Enemy surface forces attack the convoy and as extra AA and ASW protection

## SOVIET ESCORT GENERATOR

### SUMMER 1942

| D10 → | 1-6 | 7-0 |
|---|---|---|
| Lagerni to Arkangelsk | 1 Uragan TB<br>2 Aux Trawler | 2 Uragan TB,<br>2 Aux Trawler |
| Lagerni to Murmansk | 1 Liebknecht DD<br>1 Brilliant PG<br>1 Aux Trawler | 1 Project 7 DD<br>1 Uragan TB<br>1 Brilliant PG, |
| Lagerni to Kara strait | 2 Artillerist SC<br>1 Aux Trawler | 1 Brilliant PG<br>2 Artillerist SC |
| Kara strait to Murmansk | 1 Brilliant PG<br>2 Aux Trawler | 1 Liebknecht DD<br>1 Project 7 DD<br>**1 RN Halcyon AM** |

### SUMMER 1943

| D10 → | 1-6 | 7-0 |
|---|---|---|
| Lagerni to Arkangelsk | 1 Uragan TB,<br>2 Aux Trawler | 1 Liebknecht DD<br>1 Project 7 DD |
| Lagerni to Murmansk | 2 Brilliant PG,<br>1 Artillerist SC<br>**1 RN Halcyon AM** | 1 Liebknecht DD<br>3 Project 7 DD<br>1 Project 1 DD leader (Baku) |
| Lagerni to Kara strait | 2 Liebknecht DD<br>2 Artillerist SC | Brilliant PG<br>2 Artillerist SC |
| Kara strait to Murmansk | 1 Brilliant PG<br>Two Aux Trawler<br>**1 RN Halcyon AM** | 2 Uragan TB,<br>1 Brilliant PG<br>**1 RN Halcyon AM** |

### SUMMER 1944

| D10 → | 1-6 | 7-0 |
|---|---|---|
| Lagerni to Arkangelsk | 1 Liebknecht DD<br>2 Project 7 DD | 2 Project 7 DD<br>1 Uragan TB, |
| Lagerni to Murmansk | 1 Brilliant PG<br>2 ex USA YMS<br>1 Aux Trawler | 3 Project 7 DD<br>2 Uragan TB, |
| Lagerni to Kara strait | 2 Liebknecht DD<br>2 ex USA-YMS | 1 ex USA Admirable<br>2 ex USA YMS |
| Kara strait to Murmansk | 1 Project 7 DD<br>2 ex USA-YMS<br>**1 RN Halcyon AM** | 1 ex USA flush deck DD<br>3 Project 7 DD<br>1 Project 1 DD leader (Baku) |

### Spring 1945

| D10 → | 1-6 | 7-0 |
|---|---|---|
| Lagerni to Arkangelsk | 2 ex USA flush deck DD<br>2 Uragan TB, | 1 ex USA flush deck DD<br>**1 RN Algerine** |
| Lagerni to Murmansk | 2 ex USA flush deck DD<br>1 Liebknecht DD<br>2 ex USA Admirable | 2 Project 7 DD<br>3 ex USA flush deck DD<br>1 ex USA Milwaukee CL |
| Lagerni to Kara strait | 1 Brilliant PG<br>4 ex USA YMS | 1 Uragan TB<br>5 ex USA YMS |
| Kara strait to Murmansk | 1 ex USA flush deck DD<br>2 Uragan TB<br>2 ex USA Admirable | 1 ex USA flush deck DD<br>2 ex USA Admirable |

---

**SIDE NOTE**

**WHAT WAS THE SOVIET NAVY DOING?**

During the cold war era there was a tendency to play down the support provided to the Allied convoys by the Soviet Northern Fleet during the summer periods of WW2. In actual fact this was because the summer was the only time when some of the Arctic towns could be reached by sea. It was a time when these outposts had to be resupplied and produce from them picked up for delivery to mainland Russia. This all too short window of opportunity kept the Soviet Northern Fleet very busy, and being very short of ships, they were quite unable to assist with Allied convoys to any great degree.

The convoys were small and the merchant ships often very old vessels that were only active during that time of year. German action against them could be intense, many suffering heavy casualties and some being almost wiped out. British and other Allied merchant ships already in the region were occasionally used to help on these convoy runs, delivering supplies and picking up cargo for Russia. It was not a popular task because if the ships were too long delayed they could find themselves frozen in and have to spend the entire winter in Arkangelsk.

The Soviets had also been forced to ask for Allied assistance with minesweeping and local escort duty in and around the Murman coast. A group of British Halcyon class minesweepers with regular navy crews were sent and several of these units were stationed on Polyarnoe for much of the war. The facilities available for them at Polyarnoe and Murmansk were very poor and the British crews preferred to spend a lot of time at sea. Although summer was a busy time in which they worked hard at clearing mines, they were often called on to assist their hosts with escort work; hence they are occasionally shown in the Soviet escort generator. Some of the Auxiliary trawlers were ex British vessels transferred to the Soviet navy. These were mostly whale chasers, quite small and intended for minesweeping. None the less the Soviet Navy seemed happy to frequently sail them into harms way. Later the Allies transferred various other ships to the Soviet Northern Fleet. These comprised old ex USA flush deck destroyers that had already seen extensive service with the RN, the US cruiser Milwaukee (renamed Murmansk) and the Battleship HMS Royal Sovereign which was renamed Arkangelsk, but was nick named 'The Royal Rouble' by British sailors. Newly built Admirable class minesweepers and the smaller YMS type minesweepers were also transferred and well received. The transfers allowed the Soviets to operate vessels with sonar, radar and western weaponry.

Among the war materials supplied to the Soviets were radar sets, sonar / asdic and communications equipment. These were fitted to units of the Northern Fleet and unlike the Baltic and Black Sea units; there was direct contact with Allied naval personnel, who could provide valuable training and advice on the use of these new electronic equipments. In addition some ships were taken over in the UK, to where Soviet crews travelled and received direct training.

## Convoy movements

**Convoy movement is divided into two moves per day one per night**
MOVE 1 = 0401 – 1200 (Dawn until midday)
MOVE 2 = 1201 - 2000 (Midday to dusk)
MOVE 3 = 2001 - 0400 (Night)

**NOTE SOME EVENT BOXES MAY REQUIRE MORE THAN ONE ROLL PER TIME PHASE.**
Convoys roll according to the colour track they are following, and per move of the day. **If sailing to the UK, the days are still rolled for but in reverse order.**
A counter of some kind is an easy way to keep track of where your convoy is. A better way is to laminate the map, so it can be drawn on with overhead projector pens.

Fighting escort. This was deployed as shown in the following diagrams, according to the role it was currently

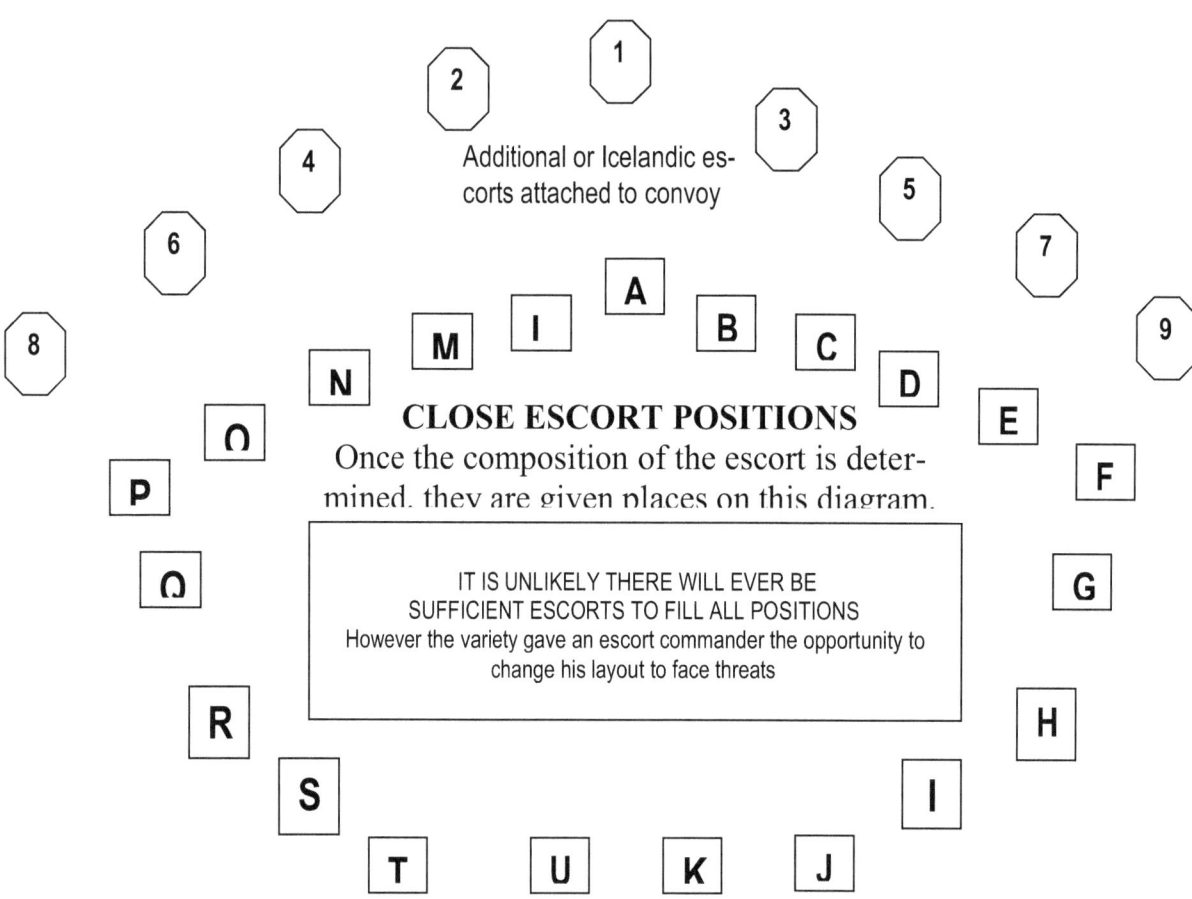

Additional or Icelandic escorts attached to convoy

## CLOSE ESCORT POSITIONS

Once the composition of the escort is determined, they are given places on this diagram.

IT IS UNLIKELY THERE WILL EVER BE
SUFFICIENT ESCORTS TO FILL ALL POSITIONS
However the variety gave an escort commander the opportunity to change his layout to face threats

## CONVOYS TO RUSSIA ESCORTS DEPLOYED AS AN ASW SCREEN

This is a typical deployment of naval escorts around a convoy to Russia. The Blue arrows show the position of the fighting escort. The larger two being cruisers. The Icelandic escorts are shown in white and are deployed ahead as an extra ASW screen. The through escort are shown in red. These ships are arranged in a much tighter screen around the convoy to provide close defence against any U Boat that slips through the other screens. Those shown in red were the positions adopted by a Western Approaches Escort Group if available. They adopted this close position because they were trained in tactics used by WA escorts and these could therefore be ordered if the situation required it. On other occasions no WA group could be spared and escorts were drawn from where ever possible, but as they therefore lacked permanent cohesion or were simply not trained in WA tactics, they were unable to perform them.

It can be appreciated from this diagram that it was extremely difficult for U Boats to reach the merchant ships and explains why losses to submarines were lower than convoys in other areas.

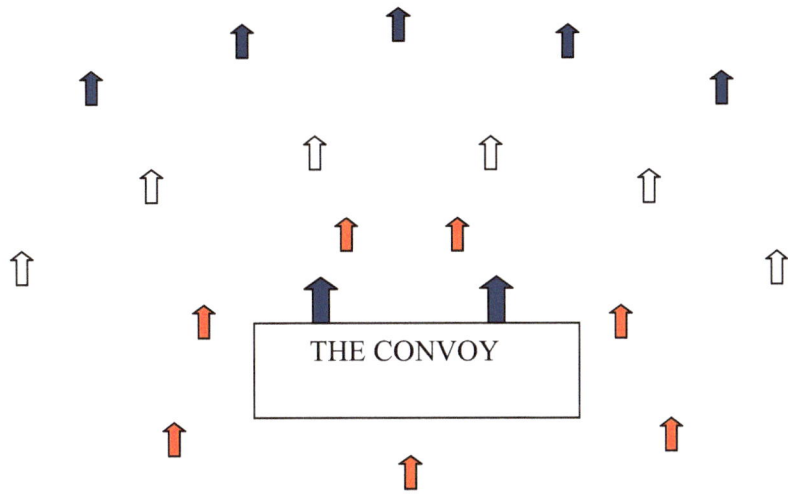

**CONVOYS TO RUSSIA ESCORTS DEPLOYED AGAINST SURFACE THREAT 1**

This formation shows how the fighting escort detaches itself from the convoy in readiness to fight off an enemy surface attack. This would be used when intelligence has warned of enemy surface ships being at sea and liable to attack the convoy. The commander can position his force to either side, behind, or to the front of the convoy depending upon where he expects the threat to come from. The forces at sea were not privy to the intelligence material available to the Admiralty, particularly ULTRA. The Admiralty plot room controlled strategic deployment and those at sea had to follow their directions. On occasion this may conflict with the opinion of the commander on the spot, but generally he would have to bow to accepting that the Admiralty may have information he did not. PQ17 was such an occasion. In that instance the Admiralty were in error but the local commander was instructed to break off with his force and proceed on a course given. The convoy itself was ordered to disperse, (Convoy will scatter) with tragic result. A task force commander would not dare to obey a direct order from the Admiralty. However if it was couched as a recommendation, it would be up to him to decide if he should follow it or not.

The fighting escort commander was responsible for not allowing enemy ships to attack the actual convoy. Therefore he had to also avoid being drawn away by an enemy contact lest another hostile warship attack from another direction. This was attempted by the Germans and had the fighting escort commander been tempted to chase his original contact, the later arrival would have had free reign against the ASW ships which were poorly armed for surface engagements. He would be aware that the Home Fleet was probably at sea somewhere, even though he was likely not to have exact information. A fleeing enemy contact was therefore not pursued because the main task was to protect the convoy, leaving destruction of the enemy to the Home Fleet. The fighting escort could only detach with the direct approval of or on direct orders from the Admiralty plot room.

The commander on the spot, was however free to engage using tactics of his own choosing.

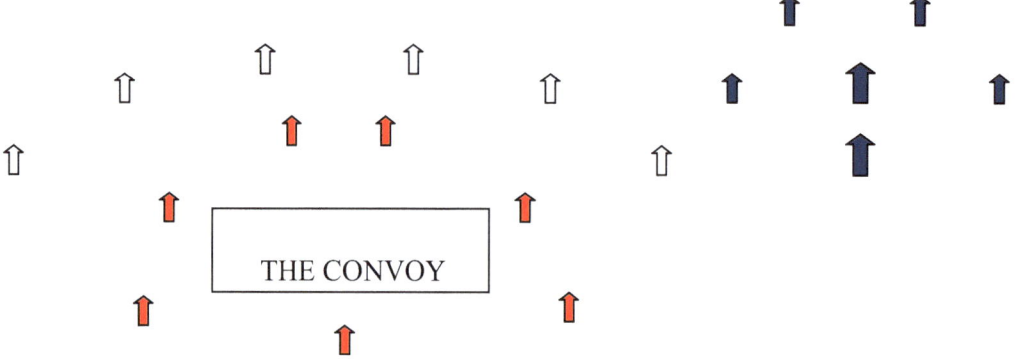

**CONVOYS TO RUSSIA ESCORTS DEPLOYED AGAINST SURFACE THREAT 2 OR AA THREAT**

This formation shows the fighting escort deployed out to one flank in response to intelligence that an enemy destroyer attack or other ships may be sent against the convoy. The fighting escort have deployed on the threatened side, but could have just as easily been put ahead, either beam, or astern of the convoy. Its position enables it to fend off a destroyer attack but is also able to counter an air attack from that side. Because of the way the ships of the fighting escort are deployed, they are still able to render some help to the ASW screen in addition to the above. Close contact allows the commander to reserve the ability to move against previously unknown threats.

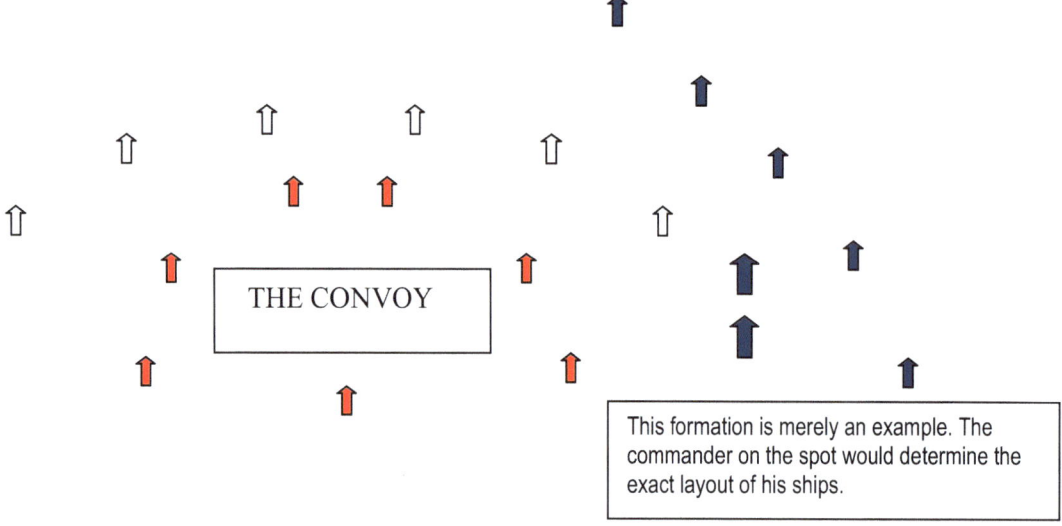

This formation is merely an example. The commander on the spot would determine the exact layout of his ships.

## CONVOYS TO RUSSIA ESCORTS DEPLOYED AS AN AA SCREEN 1

This particular formation was adopted to counter a known threat. Most of the ships have moved to the danger side and are staggered to allow a good arc of AA fire. However the close screen is keeping up their anti submarine positions to prevent a U Boat slipping in while the air attack is providing distraction. This type of defensive screen could be adopted quite quickly if the incoming attack was picked up at long range. The ability to do this was assisted by the ships of the fighting escort being fast units, able to quickly change position. The slower escort types have altered their normal position by a slower amount, while the inner screen remains in place

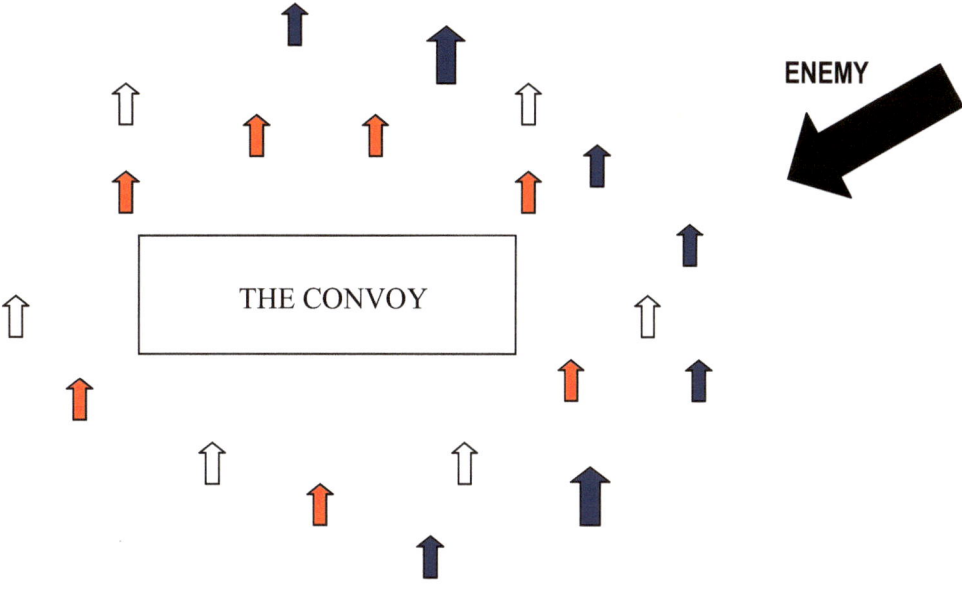

## CONVOYS TO RUSSIA ESCORTS DEPLOYED AS A CIRCULAR AA SCREEN 2

This formation shows the escorts of a convoy arranged to counter air attacks, where the likely direction of the attack is unknown. Radio intercepts often warned of enemy air activity but the direction of the attack was not known. On other occasions there might be an attack from more than one direction. This all around defence allowed the escorts to provide maximum cover regardless of the direction from which the threat arrived.

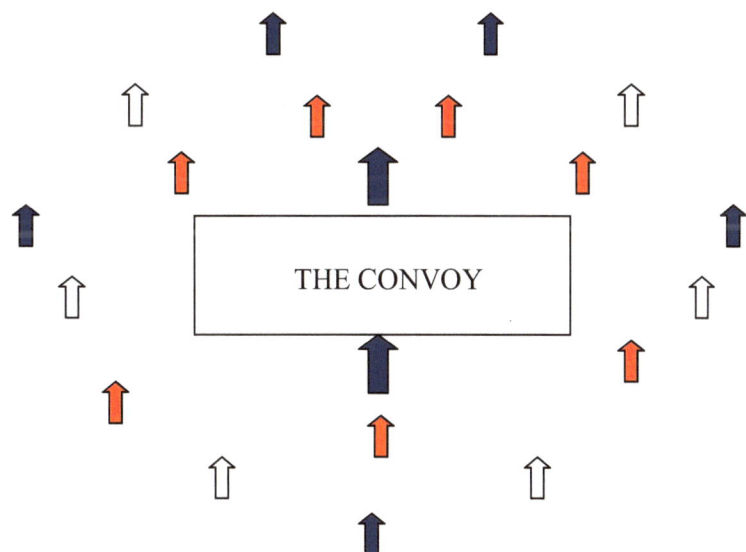

**Luftwaffe GOLDEN ZANGE (GOLDEN COMB) torpedo strikes**

This was a deadly form of torpedo attack used by He111 and Ju88 aircraft against convoys to Russia. Some of the aircraft carried two torpedoes but it was also used with single torpedo drops. The principle was that ships might avoid an individual torpedo but it would be difficult to avoid multiple threats. In addition it was realised that the convoys were heavily protected with an outer screen and to penetrate this fully would result in heavy casualties. With the golden comb, aircraft could drop one torpedo outside the outer screen, bank and drop the other one just after passing over the outer screen. The ships of the convoy would be faced by multiple torpedoes approaching from different bearings and because they were dropped further out the point of drop would be obscured. This meant it would be extremely difficult to take any form of evasive action as the ship would be unsure of which way to evade and indeed if by doing so it would not be turning into the course of another. Even warships of the screen may find they needed to move smartly to avoid being hit because there could be a threat from two or more bearings.

The Golden Comb was a mass attack method not suited for small groups. It proved effective in scoring hits but so many aircraft attacking a heavily defended convoy resulted in heavy air loss too

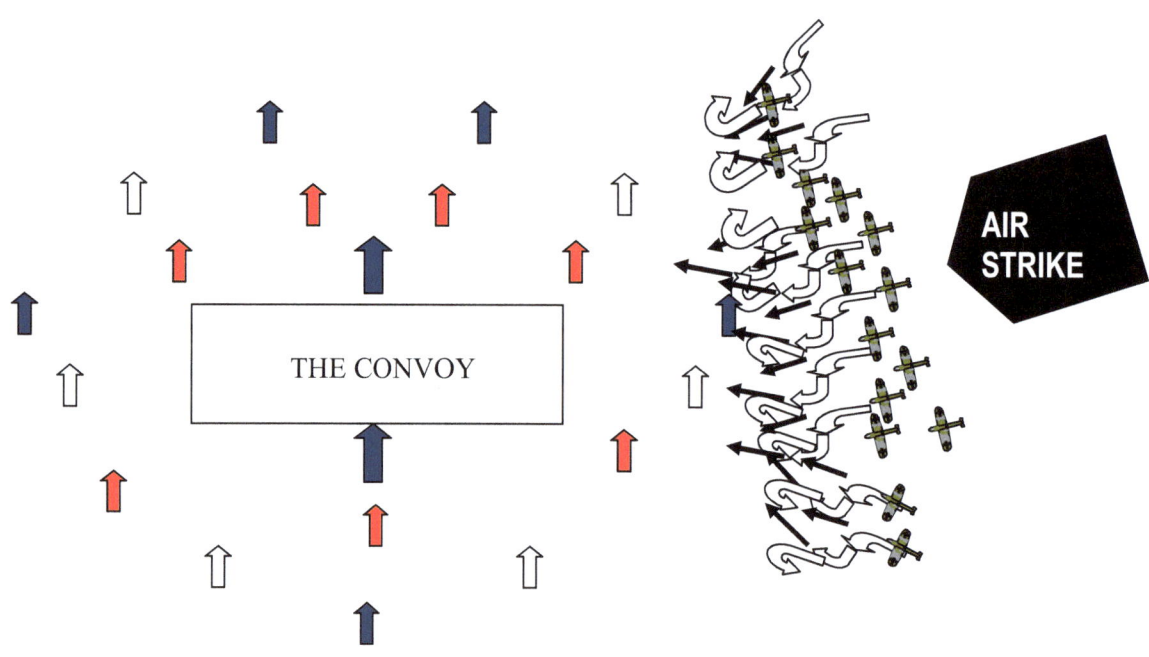

The Golden Zange was a luxury only available to the Luftwaffe when sufficient aircraft were available and with crew trained in the tactic.

Most air attacks were delivered in a much more conventional manner. In order to avoid as much flak as possible many attackers came in from the front or rear. To counter this, if one was available, the Allied convoys usually had a flak ship near the rear of the convoy. These were auxiliary AA ships converted from merchantmen and with naval crew. They were quite effective and most were faster than usual merchant ships, which enabled them to change position in the screen. If these were not available the front and rear escort positions would usually be taken up by warships with a good flak capability.

**GERMAN PLAYERS.** As with the British players, the over all strategic decisions have been taken by a higher HQ. Your concern is with the actions that will take place. At the start of the game you will roll to establish the date period. The same chart shows you the submarines available to you and a range of other vessels at sea. When contacts occur you can choose which U Boats are involved from your submarine list. If the contact is with a Blockade Runner you have a list of ships and will roll a D10 to establish which one has been spotted. As the game proceeds you will choose which submarines to commit when the event boxes call for them. You can hold back specific submarines and only commit them in certain circumstances. It's up to you. However you have no influence over the decisions of shore based high command.

**CONVOY games work best with an independent person to act as referee during tabletop battles with miniatures.**

However having performed that function over many years I can assure those who end up doing it, that the role can be a really fun one. You get to see where everyone is, what their mistakes are, and if they start actually manoeuvring around the convoy itself, it can be a load of laughs as the escorts and submarines find out that wandering around inside a convoy is like having a herd of buffalo stampeding around you. Some of my happiest wargames memories of all are of desperate battles around convoys with some daring do, from individuals and disastrous navigation from others

### CAN WE DO IT WITHOUT A REFEREE?

Yes. The game can be used without a referee as long as players can agree on various issues on non-sighted targets etc. In test play this has given fast paced, action filled games that have kept everyone on their toes.

### HOW TO PLAY

**Convoy Movement. The** days are divided into three segments.
MOVE 1. 0401 – 1200. (Dawn until midday)

MOVE 2. 1201 – 2000. (Midday to dusk)

MOVE 3. 2001 – 0400. (Night)

Convoys roll according to the colour track they are following, and per move of the day. Therefore each convoy rolls at least three times per day for event checks. On occasion they may be required to roll more than three times per day.

If sailing to the UK from Gibraltar, the days are rolled for in reverse order. From the UK to Gibraltar proceed sequentially as shown on the game map.

A counter of some kind is an easy way to keep track of where your convoy is.

**Daily Procedure**
Roll on the appropriate event chart for the first 8-hour move. Resolve events.

(1)     Roll on the appropriate event chart for the second 8-hour move. Resolve events.

(2)     Roll on the appropriate event chart for the third, or night move. Resolve events.

If an action occurs, or a ship is detached for some reason, roll D6 to determine what time this occurred in the campaign move. If a second or third event occurs, roll D6 and add to the previous time.

However an event cannot occur during the next move, therefore if more than one occurs in the last hour, then the events will be 30 minutes apart.

In addition to the above, some events may cause you to roll more than once for a specific campaign move. These still occur for the night move, even if the first was no contact.

Events that cannot occur due to weather do not take place.

Once you have selected your convoy, its route and its escorts, proceed to the map. The coloured boxes equate to which convoy you are running. The numbered boxes each represent one third of a twenty-four hour period. The number inside each coloured box indicates which event box to roll on for that campaign move. Every third box is shaded, representing a night move.

Let's presume we are running a convoy from the UK to Gibraltar. We start from near EASTOMP and the first two segments are E1 & E2. To see what happens to your convoy, you roll a D12 and refer to results in the EVENTS BOX ONE. Whatever events occur, if any, are then resolved. You then roll on E2 for events. The third box for that day is a shaded one designated NEB1. The events NIGHT EVENTS BOX ONE carries through from dusk until dawn. Most night boxes are rolled on twice. The convoy continues on its way, rolling for each event box as it occurs, until it eventually reaches its destination.

If the convoy had been proceeding to the UK from Gibraltar, it would have moved along this route in reverse order.

There are many chance factors and some of these create others, therefore no two convoys should experience the same passage, even though some events might be the same or similar on different days or nights. Some convoys will run through with very little action. The majority will have a busy time of it, and an occasional convoy will have a nightmare run, with contact after contact that will test the skill of the players for it to survive at all.

Surfaced submarines occur often during night moves. In play testing it was found best to put them on the playing area and move them in the normal manner. Until detected no ship can act against them and they therefore proceed as if the presence of the U Boat was unknown. If detected, escorts can act, but it is important to roll for each escort in position to detect. Some may fail to do so even though others have. If the detecting boat illuminates the U Boat, then others within visual range may engage it as well.

Ships with the convoy between them and a U Boat cannot use radar to detect it. If the convoy or any large ship is between or directly behind the U Boat, its own radar signature will prevent any contact by other ships. In general the detecting ship needs the area behind the U Boat to be clear of other obstructions. This should also apply to visual sighting when a U Boat is close to the convoy.

Combat between the convoy, aircraft, U-boats or surface ships, is carried out using the combat resolution rules provided. I recommend the use of the torpedo markers. In the majority of cases the torpedo will reach its target in a single move, and if not sighted there will be no evasive action. Therefore players can simply proceed straight to determination of hits and damage resolution.

Gunnery does not occur a lot. However submarines forced to the surface or surprised can be engaged with guns. Some are quite ineffective but the principle was to engage with a storm of fire, using all the light guns a ship carried as well as its larger armament. This was intended to drive the crew away from their deck guns, and prevent the command crew carrying out their duties. It was also used to stop crew abandoning a damaged boat, in that hope that in doing so, they would choose to save their lives by not scuttling. Captured boats provided vital intelligence. Because only a few ships are likely to be involved in a gunnery action, it has been possible to include guns from machinegun size upward.

| Date and D10 roll | U Boats Available | Surface Ships Available |
|---|---|---|
| (1) January - June 1942 | 8 x Type II. 3 x Type VIIB, 3 x Type VIIC | Lutzow, Nuremberg, Köln, Z4, Z5, Z6, Z7, Z10, Z23, Z25, Z26, Z27, T15, T16, T17, 6 x M Boote. 2 x Auxiliary minelayer. |
| (2) July – December 1942 | 8 x Type II. 3 x Type VIIB, 2 x Type VIIC | Tirpitz, Scharnhorst Admiral Scheer, Admiral Hipper, Prinz Eugen, Z4, Z5, Z6, Z10, Z14, Z16, Z20, Z27, Z28, Z29, Z30, T20, T21. 2xAuxiliary minelayer |
| (3-4) January - June 1943 | 6 x Type II. 1 x Type VIIB, 4 x Type VIIC | Tirpitz, Admiral Scheer, Z4, Z5, Z6, Z10 Z14, Z20, Z24, Z29, Z30, Z31, Z33, T20, T21. 2 x Auxiliary minelayer |
| (5-6) July – December 1943 | 6 x Type II. 1 x Type VIIB, 12 x Type VIIC | Tirpitz, Scharnhorst, Admiral Scheer, Admiral Hipper, Z4, Z6, Z10, Z28, Z29, Z30, Z31, Z33, Z34, Z38, T20, T21.T28. |
| (7) January - June 1944 | 1 x Type VIIB, 18 x Type VIIC | Tirpitz, Admiral Scheer, Z29, Z30, Z31, Z33, Z34, Z38, T28. Auxiliary minelayer |
| (8) July – December 1944 | 1 x Type VIIB, 20 x Type VIIC | Tirpitz, Admiral Scheer, Z29, Z31, Z33, Z34, Z38, Auxiliary minelayer |
| (9) January – February 1945 | 1 x Type VIIB, 25 x Type VIIC | Admiral Scheer Lutzow until February, Z33, Z34, Z38, |
| (0) March – May 1945 | 1 x Type XXIII, 20 x Type VIIC, 2 x type XXI. | Z31, Z33. |

**German Auxiliary Minelayers** were usually converted from merchant ships. They were quite active in northern waters.

In addition to the ships and submarines listed, there were also a large number of depot ships, auxiliary minesweepers, escorts and coastal craft. They are not listed as they play no role in Arctic Storm.

**U Boats.** After the crucial battles of mid 1943 many U Boats were withdrawn from Atlantic operations and sent to Norway. Many of these kept their deck gun as the reduced danger from aircraft meant there were opportunities to use such a weapon. This especially applied during operations off the Soviet Arctic coast. Although large numbers were available they proved less effective than expected. Freezing conditions were just as bad for the U Boat crews as for ships and heavy weather made for difficulty in interception. One unusual problem faced by them in the frigid air was that their diesel exhaust fumes formed a very visible cloud of smoke, which in several encounters made it easy for Allied escorts to see them while on the surface. The severe conditions caused many machinery and equipment problems with the result that many boats were under repair, or forced to return for repairs after relatively short patrols.

They were also faced with a more developed technology than in earlier years and the loss of so many crews earlier in the war, meant that most boats were manned with very inexperienced men. In general they performed well against the Soviet Navy, but less so against the Western Allies, who were a very practiced and experienced group.

The number of U Boats allocated above represents those available for action with reasonably trained crew. There were far more stationed in Norway, but the majority were engaged in training. The Germans, having realised the standard boats were no longer effective, were placing their hopes on the new types under construction. When these entered service in numbers it was intended to renew the U Boat offensive. Thus existing crews were being preserved for when the new boats would be available.

## SIGHTINGS AND BEARINGS

**RED = Port. (Left)**
**GREEN = Starboard. (Right).**

The direction of a sighting, were described as red or green, followed by a degree from the bow of the ship.

For example. 'Ship bearing RED 90. Range 3 miles'. This would indicate that there was a ship at 3 miles range on the port side and ninety degrees from the bow of the sighting ship.

'Aircraft. GREEN 30, low two miles'. Would indicate an aircraft 30 degrees from the starboard bow, low down and two miles distant.

The sequence told all other lookouts and officers firstly what to look for, which side of the ship, what angle of bearing, and lastly how far away. If the lookout was able to do so he would also add more detail such as if the sighting was unknown, an enemy, or friendly.

**In this game, all sightings use the above system.**

| D10 | Daylight    WINTER EVENTS BOX Daylight D1 | Result |
|---|---|---|
| 1-6 | **No enemy contact** Convoy proceeds. | Proceed |
| 7 | **MINE** One ship, merchant ship has struck a floating mine. *Weather light fog Choppy seas* | Resolve |
| 8 | **COLLISION** One merchant ship has collided with an escort during assembly of the convoy. Roll for which ships affected. Decide on ships remaining with the convoy or not depending on damage. | Resolve |
| 9 | **COLLISION.** One merchant ship has collided with another during assembly of the convoy. Decide on ships remaining with the convoy or not depending on damage | Combat |
| 0 | **ENEMY RECON.** After the convoy has formed up a German He177 reconnaissance aircraft with radar circles it at very high level beyond gunnery range and transmits message to its base. *Weather Visibility low. Very rough seas.* Unable to launch aircraft. | Proceed |

| D10 | Daylight    WINTER    EVENTS BOX Daylight D2  *If German aircraft in contact last move* **add 3 to die roll** | |
|---|---|---|
| 1-4 | **No enemy contact.** Convoy proceeds | Proceed |
| 5 | **ENGINEERING.** One Destroyer suffers machinery defects and is forced to turn back. It will rejoin at the end of day 4. NOTE RETURN. | Resolve |
| 6 | **SMOKEY JOE.** One ship making excessive smoke. Roll on this event box again and add 3 to die | Resolve |
| 7-0 | **AIR ATTACK.** Roll on air attack table 1. **Incoming aircraft detected at long range bearing NNE.** If CAP present it can intercept or CAM ship may launch fighter. **U Boat** in submerged position bearing green 30 at range 2000yds from starboard most ship of the close escort screen. ALLIES test for detection. **Un-detected submerged U Boat** in attack position bearing red 45 at range 3000yds from leading ship of the fighting escort screen. This U Boat may fire at once if wished. *Weather clear visibility, choppy seas visibility 12nm* | AAT-1 Resolve Combat |

| D10 | WINTER EVENTS BOX    Arctic twilight. TW 1 | |
|---|---|---|
| 1-6 | **No enemy contact.** Convoy proceeds in low visibility and choppy seas | Proceed |
| 7 | *HEAVY WEATHER, low cloud.* All further rolls this day **& coming night cancelled.** Proceed to 1st move of next day | Proceed |
| 8 | **BREAKDOWN.** Merchant Ship has suffered major engineering failure. Detach one escort to tow it back to nearest port | Resolve |
| 9 | **BREAKDOWN.** One Cruiser or fleet destroyer in the fighting escort has suffered a major engineering failure and must be detached with an escort to return it to base at a maximum of 10 knots. *Weather. Visibility 2nm. Seas rough* | Resolve |
| 0 | **U BOAT** on surface close to convoy, bearing red 90 from leading close escort port side, range 3nm. ALLIES test for detection. *Heavy weather* and rough seas. Visibility 2nm. Wind medium from NNE. **Roll on this event box again** Ships with radar 285 may engage outside visibility | Combat |

| D10 | WINTER EVENTS BOX    Arctic twilight. TW 2 | |
|---|---|---|
| 1-7 | **No enemy contact.** Convoy proceeds in low visibility and choppy seas | Proceed |
| 8 | **SURPRISE. U Boat on surface** visually sighted surfacing on bearing green 145 at range 2500yds from rear ship of the close escort. U Boat also sights the escort. Mutual surprise. German first move. *Weather Very cold. Slight seas light snow. Light NE wind. Visibility 2500yds* | Combat |
| 9 | **U Boat submerged** bearing green 90 at range 4000yds from first ship in the column one. ALLIES test for detection. *Weather choppy seas, sleet, extreme cold, low cloud, strong SE wind, visibility 3nm* | Combat |
| 0 | **WEATHER.** *Very Heavy seas low cloud and sleet.* Convoy undetected. All further rolls this day **& coming night cancelled.** Proceed to 1st move of next day. **Ships that have suffered floatation damage** roll for a further minor flooding and control | Proceed |

| D10 | WINTER EVENTS BOX    Arctic twilight. TW 3 | |
|---|---|---|
| 1-6 | **CONVOY Rendezvous point met.** Local escort detached and proceed to Seidisfjord. Convoy proceeds with through escort | Proceed |
| 7 | **CONVOY Rendezvous point met.** If the convoy was previous sighted or attacked by U boats or aircraft, Roll once on **Air Attack** Table 1. Raid fails to find the main convoy and will attack the local escort that detached for Seidisfjord. *Weather Mild seas. Icy cold. Visibility 2nm. Slight NW wind.* High or medium Raid detected at maximum radar range. Low level at 3nm. Ships with radar 285 may engage outside visibility. | Combat |
| 6-8 | **CONVOY Rendezvous point met.** Two merchant ships collide. If unable to continue they will proceed to Reykjavik with the departing local escort. *Weather Rough seas.* Visibility 4nm. | Combat |
| 9 | **CONVOY Rendezvous missed.** Un-detected U Boat submerged in attack position bearing green 40 at range 2000yds from third ship in the starboard column. Sonar effectiveness of all ships reduced by 1. *Weather* Choppy seas. Visibility 4 nm. **Roll on this event box again until rendezvous met. Roll on next night box twice as convoy is now behind schedule** | Combat |
| 10 | **CONVOY Rendezvous met but delayed by severe weather conditions.** Local escort detached and proceed to Seidisfjord. Convoy proceeds with through escort. Roll on the next event box (N4) twice instead of once unless cancelled out by previous event roll on TW 2 | Proceed |

| D10 | WINTER EVENTS BOX — Arctic twilight. TW 4 | |
|---|---|---|
| 1-4 | **GROWLERS.** Convoy enters floating ice field. Ships with previous floatation damage suffer automatic minor flooding and roll for control. *Weather* Clear, mild seas Light SE wind, Icy cold. **HOME FLEET.** Roll on the Home Fleet Arctic twilight box **REFUELING** may be carried out | Proceed |
| 5 | **WEATHER.** Sleet and extreme seas. Gale force winds from NW. Visibility 500yds. All ships stream collision buoys. Test roll 1-5 on D10 for collision between first and second ships of a column. Roll for which. **REFUELING** not possible. | Resolve |
| 6 | **WEATHER.** Sleet and very heavy seas. Full Gale from NW. Visibility 500yds. One merchant ship damaged by heavy seas and cargo shift. Test for major flooding **REFUELING not possible.** Ships unable to refuel must detach to Siedisfjord and will not return to the convoy. | Resolve |
| 7-8 | **Submerged U Boat detected** bearing green 10 at range 2000 yds from leading ship of fighting escort. *Weather.* Mild seas. Icy cold. Moderate wind from North. Visibility 3nm Sonar conditions excellent + 1 to all ASDIC and Sonar sets. **ULTRA** message from Admiralty. German warships have sailed from Norway. Die rolls on TW 6 now add +3. **REFUELING** may be carried out | Resolve |
| 9-0 | **WEATHER.** *Choppy seas low cloud and sleet.* Convoy undetected. All further rolls this day & coming night cancelled. Proceed to 1st move of next day. **Ships that have suffered floatation damage** roll for a further minor flooding and control. **REFUELING** may be carried out | Proceed |

| D10 | WINTER EVENTS BOX — Arctic twilight. TW 5 | |
|---|---|---|
| 1-3 | **No enemy contact.** Convoy proceeds in low visibility, extreme cold and moderate seas **REFUELING** may be carried out | Proceed |
| 4 | **ENGINEERING.** One ship of the fighting escort is suffering condenseritis. Maximum speed reduced to half. Unable to repair at sea **WEATHER.** *Extreme cold and choppy seas.* **REFUELING** may be carried out | Resolve |
| 5 | **SERIOUS FIRE** has broken out on board one merchant ship. Roll again 2 for this event box at +2 due to visible smoke. **RE-INFORCEMENTS.** SEG 4 joins close escort. **WEATHER.** *Extreme cold and strong swell.* **REFUELING** may be carried out | Resolve |
| 6-7 | **AIR ATTACK. Roll on Air Attack table 2.** High or medium Raid detected at maximum radar range approaching from North. **CAM** ship may launch. **CAP** can intercept outside AA range. **Carrier** launches 3 fighters to intercept inside long AA range. Low level Raid detected at visibility. *Weather* clear twilight. Calm seas. Extreme cold. Visibility 6nm. **HOME FLEET.** Roll on the Home Fleet Arctic twilight box. **REFUELING** may be carried out | Combat |
| 8 | **ULTRA message from Admiralty.** German warships have sailed from Norway. **Die rolls on TW 6 now +3.** One merchant ship becomes a straggler during heavy storm. Test on Events Beyond Convoy table. **REFUELING** not possible. | Proceed |
| 8 | **GROWLERS.** Convoy encounters heavy floating ice pack. *Speed* of all ships reduced to half their normal. One Escort suffers Radar breakdown due to ice. Unable to repair. **AIR ATTACK.** Roll on Air Attack table 3. High or medium Raid detected at maximum radar range approaching from astern. **CAP** may intercept outside AA range. No launch from Carrier due to icing. Low level detected at maximum visibility astern. *Weather.* Extreme cold and icing. Light wind from NE. Visibility 4 nm calm seas All AA factors reduced by half due to icing. **REFUELING** may be carried out | Resolve |
| 0 | **RADAR CONTACT. Unknown ship** bearing green 45, range 12 miles. Fighting escort already deployed in battle formation on contact side of the convoy if admiralty warning previously received. Detach to intercept. *Weather.* Visibility 5nm Sea state choppy. Strong wind from NW. All gunnery and Torpedo factors reduced by half due to icing and conditions. Roll on **ISB2**. Also roll on HF1 Box | Resolve |

| D10 | WINTER EVENTS BOX     Arctic twilight. TW 6 | |
|---|---|---|
| 1-4 | **No enemy contact**. Convoy proceeds. SEG 5 joins the close escort. **ULTRA message from Admiralty**. German warships have sailed from Norway. | |
| 5 | **AIR ATTACK**. Roll on Air Attack table 3. *Cloud base low Air attacks at medium must attack from low. Air attacks at high will abort.* Raid detected at maximum radar range. **CAM** ship may launch fighter for intercept at long AA range. Carrier cannot launch due to rough seas and icing **Weather**. *Extreme cold. Strong wind from north. Visibility 2 nm.* Scout aircraft will illuminate target. Ships with radar 285 may engage outside visibility **Surfaced U Boat detected** bearing green 140 at range 5000 yds from rear ship of close escort | Resolve |
| 6-7 | **AIR ATTACK**. Roll on Air Attack table2. *Raid undetected if low level. Other detected at maximum range.* Roll on Soviet/Allied **ADTL** *Cloud base medium. High attacks will abort.* **Weather**. *Extreme cold. Visibility 1 nm. Choppy seas. Strong wind from SW.* Scout aircraft will illuminate targets. Ships with radar 285 may engage outside visibility **Submerged U Boat** bearing red 170 from rear ship of the centre column at range 2000yds | Proceed |
| 8 | **RE-INFORCEMENTS**. Two British Halcyon class minesweepers of the Kola local escort group join the close escort | Proceed |
| 9 | **AIR ATTACK**. Roll Air Attack table 3. *Cloud base medium Air attacks at high will attack from medium.* Raid detected at maximum radar range. No surprise for low level. *Roll on Soviet/Allied ASTL for fighter cover.* **Weather**. *Extreme cold, visibility 1 nm, choppy seas. Slight wind from SE.* Scout aircraft will illuminate targets. Reduce AA factors by half due to heavy icing. Ships with radar 285 may engage outside visibility **Undetected Submerged U Boat** bearing red 145 from rear ship column one range 1500yds Sonar condition poor reduce detection by 2. Soviet MRB patrol aircraft 3nm behind convoy. | Resolve |
| 0 | **RADAR CONTACT unknown ship** bearing green 90, range 9 miles. Fighting escort already deployed in battle formation on contact side of the convoy if admiralty warning previously received. Detach to intercept. **Weather**. *Visibility 3 nm. Sea state heavy seas. Snow squalls. High winds from North. Speed of Destroyers and smaller ships reduced to 20 knots maximum.* All destroyer gunnery and torpedo factors reduced by half due to icing and conditions. Cruisers and larger not effected. Roll on **ISB-1**. Also roll on HF5 | Resolve |
| | WINTER EVENTS BOX     Arctic twilight. TW 7 | |
| 1-3 | **ARRIVAL**. Convoy enters Kola inlet without further incident. | Resolve |
| 4 | **MINE**. Convoy enters Kola inlet. One merchant ship strikes a mine. | Resolve |
| 5 | **MINE**. Convoy enters Kola inlet. One close escort strikes a mine. | Resolve |
| 6 | **MINES**. Convoy enters Kola inlet. One close escort and one merchant ship strike mines. | Resolve |
| 7 | **ARRIVAL**. Convoy enters Kola inlet. SEG 2 joins convoy. **AIR ATTACK**. Roll on Air Attack table 4 *Roll on Soviet/Allied AST for fighter cover.* **Weather**. *Extreme cold. Very clear. Light wind from SE. No clouds. Visibility 6 nm.* | Combat |
| 8 | **ARRIVAL**. Convoy enters Kola inlet. Fighting escort detached to Polyarnoe. After fighting escort detached **AIR ATTACK**. Roll on Air Attack table 4. *Roll on Soviet/Allied AST for fighter cover.* **Weather**. *Extreme cold. High cloud. Visibility 4 nm.* Convoy and close escorts in single file, following Soviet ice breaker through thin pack ice. All merchant ship AA factors reduced by half due to icing. Warships not effected. | Combat |
| 9-0 | Convoy enters Kola inlet. Fighting escort detached to Polyarnoe. SEG 3 joins convoy. Roll on **AIR ATTACK** table 4. *Roll on Soviet/Allied AST for fighter cover.* **Weather**. *Extreme cold. Light snow. Visibility 2nm.* | Combat |
| D10 | WINTER EVENTS BOX N1     ARCTIC NIGHT | |
| 1-8 | **No enemy contact.** Convoy proceeds | Resolve |
| 9 | **MINES**. Convoy sails into drifting mines. Roll 1-2 = no ships struck. 3-6 = one merchant struck hit. 7-8 two merchant struck.<br>9 = one destroyer of fighting escort struck. 0 = Larger warship of fighting escort struck. | Resolve |
| 0 | **Panic**. One merchant ship panics, and fires a snowflake illuminant rocket to starboard of convoy. **Axis player** may attack with 1 surfaced submarine of choice from 4,000yds and starboard bearing of choice against any visible illuminated ship of the close escort. **WEATHER** sleet rain, rough sea, strong wind from NE, visibility 500yds but illuminated range 6000yds. | Combat |
| | WINTER EVENTS BOX N2     ARCTIC NIGHT | |
| 1-6 | **No enemy contact.** Convoy proceeds | |
| 7-8 | **German U Boat submerged** on bearing RED 90, 750yds from lead ship of column one. Allies test for detection. **WEATHER**. *Aurora illuminates the area in artificial daylight. Visibility 5nm. Seas slight. Slight wind from NE. Intense cold* | Combat |
| 9 | **Undetected U boat submerged** on bearing RED 90, 450yds from second ship of column one. **WEATHER** *heavy sleet, choppy sea and high winds from NNE. Visibility 500yds.* Test for detection and combat. All gunnery and ASW factors reduced by half due to icing and conditions | Combat |
| 0 | **German U Boat** submerged. Detected on bearing red 45, 1500yds from the leading portside close escort of convoy. **WEATHER**. *Aurora illuminates the area in artificial daylight. Visibility 7nm. Seas choppy. Slight wind fro NE. Intense cold* | Combat |

| D10 | WINTER EVENTS BOX N3    ARCTIC NIGHT | Result |
|---|---|---|
| 1-4 | **No enemy contact.** Convoy proceeds. Do not make normal second roll unless required by previous events effect | |
| 5 | **U Boat surprised and sighted** visually, while surfacing 250yds red 45 from leading escort. **WEATHER.** Visibility 500yds. Seas rough. Sleet and high winds from North. All gunnery and ASW factors reduced by half due to icing and conditions | Combat |
| 6 | **U Boat undetected** comes to periscope depth between ships of column 3 and 4. **WEATHER.** Aurora floods the area in artificial daylight. All ships brightly illuminated. Visibility 7nm. Seas choppy. Slight wind from NNW. Intense cold | Combat |
| 7 | **U Boat submerged** between ships of columns 5 & 6. **WEATHER.** Visibility average. Choppy seas. Strong wind from NNE. One merchant ship a straggler. Refer EBC chart | Combat |
| 8 | **Collision.** Rear ship of a column has collided with the stern of the ship ahead of it. Both ships will be stationary until dawn, in addition to any damage rolled. At least one escort must sweep around them for protection while situation is resolved; if either ship is abandoned refer to EBC chart. **WEATHER.** Visibility 500yds. Seas rough. Sleet and high winds. All gunnery and ASW factors reduced by half due to icing and conditions | Resolve |
| 9-0 | **EARLY RENDEZVOUS** Icelandic and UK sections of convoy meet earlier than expected. Do not roll on TW3. Proceed straight to next night. On roll of 1-8 union of convoy and detachment of local escort takes place without incident. On roll of 9-0 the local escort will engage arriving ships of the through escort for two moves with gunnery at range 4nm due to mistaken identity. Arriving ships will not return fire. Convoy then proceeds as above | Resolve |
| | WINTER EVENTS BOX N4    ARCTIC NIGHT | |
| 1-3 | **No enemy contact.** Convoy proceeds | Proceed |
| 4 | **WEATHER** Severe squalls. High seas. Poor visibility. **Ships with floatation damage** develop serious flooding and must check for control. One merchant ship and one of the close escorts lose touch and become stragglers. Roll for which. See EBC chart | Resolve. |
| 5 | **FIRE.** Merchant ship has a critical fire on board. Roll for which ship. **If fire lasts 3 moves** ship blows up and sinks unless reduced to minor. **Roll on this event box again with +4 to die**. If contact takes place the ship will still be illuminated by fire See EBC chart if ship is forced to be abandoned in damaged state | Resolve |
| 6-8 | **Submerged U Boat** detected on ASDIC at *periscope* 900yds Red 25 from lead escort on port side. **Weather.** *Extreme cold. Light wind. Visibility 1 nm calm sea. Snow squalls.* **Warships** may not exceed 15 knots due to presence of growlers. | Combat |
| 9 | **GROWLERS.** Convoy encounters heavy floating ice pack. *Speed* of all ships reduced to 5 knots. One Escort suffers ASDIC/Sonar breakdown due to ice. Unable to repair. **AIR ATTACK.** Roll on Air Attack table 1. Due to severe icing the raid is not detected on radar. **Weather.** *Extreme cold. Light wind. Visibility 1 nm calm sea.* All AA factors reduced by half due to icing. Type 285 radar ineffective due to floe returns and icing. Air attack will use scouts to illuminate targets | Resolve |
| 0 | **WOLF PACK IN CONTACT WITH CONVOY.** Three type VIIC U Boats on surface at the following ranges. Bearing Red 20 at range 2500 yds from port wing ship of fighting escort. Bearing green 100 at range 3000 yds from the rear most escort. Bearing Green 45 at range 4500 yds from first ship of starboard column of convoy. Closest one can fire immediately. Escorts check for detection of others. **Weather.** *Extreme cold. Light wind. Visibility 5000yds calm sea.* **Check escorts for contact** | Combat |
| | WINTER EVENTS BOX N5    ARCTIC NIGHT | |
| 1-3 | **No enemy contact.** Convoy proceeds. REFUELING. One destroyer of the close escort must refuel during the next twilight period. If unable to do so it must detach and proceed independently, direct to Polyarnoe | Resolve |
| 4 | **ICE DAMAGE.** One ship of the close escort has collided with a growler. Asdic lost until harbour repair. Serious flooding | Resolve |
| 5 | **ICE DAMAGE.** One destroyer of the fighting escort has collided with a growler. Asdic lost until harbour repair. Serious flooding | Resolve |
| 6 | **GERMAN AIRCRAFT** detected in contact with the convoy. Aircraft circles convoy outside gunnery range throughout the night using radar to stay in contact. CAM ship or CVE cannot launch interceptor. Add 3 to die roll for next events box **Weather.** *Extreme cold. Light wind. Visibility 5000yds calm sea.* | Resolve |
| 7 | **ICE DAMAGE.** One merchant ship strikes large growler. Speed reduced to 5 knots and major flooding. One escort must be detached to assist. Refer to EBC table for fate. **HOME FLEET.** Also roll on the Home fleet night events box | Resolve |
| 8 | **Panic.** One merchant ship panics and fires tracers at false air target. Convoy sighted. Roll on AAT 1. **Weather.** *Extreme cold. Light wind from NW. Visibility 5000yds calm sea* | Combat |
| 9-0 | **INVESTIGATE A SIGHTING.** Radar contact at maximum range from leading ship of fighting escort. **Roll on ISB1.** Fighting escort already deployed in battle formation on contact side of the convoy if admiralty warning previously received. Detach to intercept **Weather.** *Extreme cold. Light wind from NNE. Visibility 3000yds calm sea. Visibility with illumination is 9000yds.* **Also roll on HF10** | Combat |

| D10 | WINTER EVENTS BOX N6 — ARCTIC NIGHT | Result |
|---|---|---|
| 1-3 | No enemy contact. Convoy proceeds | |
| 4 | **WEATHER.** Aurora illuminates the area in bright artificial daylight. Visibility 6nm. Seas choppy. Slight wind from NNW. Intense cold. Due to severe icing all AA factors reduced to half. Roll on AAT 3. No illumination required. **REFUELING.** One destroyer may use the bright conditions to refuel instead of during twilight | Combat |
| 5 | **ICE DAMAGE.** One ship of the close escort has collided with a growler. Asdic lost until harbour repair. Serious flooding speed reduced to a maximum of ten knots. **HOME FLEET.** Also roll on the Home fleet night events box | Resolve |
| 6 | **ICE PACK.** Edge of ice pack encountered unexpectedly. **Leading close escort** on the port side of convoy seriously damaged. Major flooding, propellers wrecked. Must be taken under tow. Two merchant ships of port column collide while avoiding ice. Use collision table. If Soviet icebreaker present a warning is given and this event does not occur. | Resolve |
| 7 | **SOVIET SEG 1.** joins the convoy. Add to close screen | Resolve |
| 8 | **BRITISH.** Two Halcyon class minesweepers join from Murmansk. Place with close escort | Resolve |
| 9 | **GERMAN AIRCRAFT** is detected in contact with the convoy. Aircraft circles convoy outside gunnery range throughout the night using radar to stay in contact. CAM ship or CVE cannot launch interceptor. Add 4 to die roll for next TW events box. | Resolve |
| 0 | **INVESTIGATE A SIGHTING.** Radar contact at maximum range from leading ship of fighting escort. **Roll on ISB1.** Fighting escort already deployed in battle formation on contact side of the convoy if admiralty warning previously received. Detach to intercept | Resolve |

| D10 | ISB-1 — INVESTIGATE A SIGHTING BOX 1 WINTER | Time taken | Action |
|---|---|---|---|
| 1-2 | Identified as a fast **SOVIET** icebreaker searching for the convoy. Place at head of screen | 1 EV box | Resolve |
| 3 | **SOVIET** independent sailing freighter lost due to damage to navigation equipment. Escort it to the convoy | 1 EV box | Resolve |
| 4 | **ALLIED** merchant ship on fast independent sailing route from Murmansk | 1/2 EV box | |
| 5 | **ALLIED** Light Cruiser on fast independent sailing despatch duty, outbound from Polyarnoe | 1/2 EV box | Resolve |
| 6 | **ALLIED** merchant ship. 50% sinking condition engines out of action. Rescue survivors and scuttle ship | 1 EV box | Resolve |
| 7 | **SOVIET** warships searching for convoy **SEG 6** joins fighting escort | 1 EV box | |
| 8-9 | **ENEMY** warships identified at range 10nm. Roll on **GERMAN CONTACT CHART**. Also on HOME FLEET **HF-1** | 1 EV box | COMBAT |

### WINTER GERMAN CONTACT CHART

| D10 | 1942 | 1943 | 1944 | 1945 | Result |
|---|---|---|---|---|---|
| 1-2 | Auxiliary minelayer | Auxiliary minelayer and 3 DD | Auxiliary minelayer | | Combat |
| 3-4 | Auxiliary minelayer and 2 DD | Admiral Scheer and Admiral Hipper | 3 DD | 2 DD minelaying mission | Combat |
| 5-6 | 3 DD minelaying mission | Prinz Eugen and 4 DD | 5 DD | 2 large DD | Combat |
| 7-8 | 5 large DD | Scharnhorst unaccompanied | Admiral Scheer | 2 large DD | Combat |
| 9 | Lutzow and 3 DD | Scharnhorst and 4 DD | Tirpitz unaccompanied | DD | Combat |
| 0 | Nuremberg, Köln and 4DD | Tirpitz and four large DD | Tirpitz and 4 DD | | Combat |

| Date | GERMAN U Boats | GERMAN Available surface Ships |
|---|---|---|
| January – June 1942 | 8 Type II. 3 Type VIIB, 3 Type VIIC | Lutzow, Nuremberg, Köln, Z4, Z5, Z6, Z7, Z10, Z23, Z25, Z26, Z27, T15, T16, T17, 6 x M Boote. 2 x Auxiliary minelayer. |
| July – Dec 1942 | 8 Type II. 3 Type VIIB, 2 Type VIIC | Tirpitz, Scharnhorst Admiral Scheer, Admiral Hipper, Prinz Eugen, Z4, Z5, Z6, Z10, Z14, Z16, Z20, Z27, Z28, Z29, Z30, T20, T21. 2xAuxiliary minelayer |
| January – June 1943 | 6 Type II. 1 Type VIIB, 4 Type VIIC | Tirpitz, Admiral Scheer, Z4, Z5, Z6, Z10 Z14, Z20, Z24, Z29, Z30, Z31, Z33, T20, T21. 2 x Auxiliary minelayer |
| July – Dec 1943 | 6 Type II. 1 Type VIIB, 12 Type VIIC | Tirpitz, Scharnhorst, Admiral Scheer, Admiral Hipper, Z4, Z6, Z10, Z28, Z29, Z30, Z31, Z33, Z34, Z38, T20, T21.T28. |
| January – June 1944 | 1 Type VIIB, 18 Type VIIC | Tirpitz, Admiral Scheer, Z29, Z30, Z31, Z33, Z34, Z38, T28. Auxiliary minelayer |
| July – Dec 1944 | 1 Type VIIB, 20 Type VIIC | Tirpitz, Admiral Scheer, Z29, Z31, Z33, Z34, Z38, Auxiliary minelayer |
| January – Feb 1945 | 1 Type VIIB, 25 Type VIIC | Admiral Scheer Lutzow until February, Z33, Z34, Z38, |
| March – May 1945 | 1 Type XXIII, 20 Type VIIC, 2 type XXI. | Z31, Z33. |

| D10 | HM 1.  HOME FLEET.  WINTER |
|---|---|
| 1-2 | Home fleet too far away to assist. |
| 3 | Home fleet can launch **air strike Y** to assist and arriving on tactical combat move twenty (60 minutes) of surface action taking place during a twilight move. If night contact HF is unable to assist at all. |
| 4 | Home fleet has already detached **CF A** which will arrive from the south on tactical combat move nine (27 minutes) of any action taking place. The rest of the HF is too far away to assist. |
| 5 | Home fleet has already detached **CF B** which will arrive from the south on tactical combat move nine (27 minutes) of any action taking place. |
| 6-7 | Home fleet has already detached **CF C** which will arrive from the south on tactical combat move five (15 minutes) of any action taking place. Home fleet can launch two air strikes to assist, arriving on tactical combat move five (15 minutes) **air strike Z** and twelve (36 minutes) **air strike X** of surface action taking place during a twilight move. If any enemy unit slowed to 20 knots or less HF B will arrive within twenty tactical combat moves of action taking place. (60 minutes) |
| 8-9 | Home fleet has been tracking the enemy force. **HF force B** will arrive ten moves (30 minutes) after combat commences. |
| 0 | Home fleet has been tracking the enemy force. **HF force A** will arrive ten moves (30 minutes) after combat commences. |

| D10 | WINTER HOME FLEET EVENTS BOX    Arctic twilight | ACTION |
|---|---|---|
| 1-4 | No enemy contact.. **ULTRA message from Admiralty.** German warships have sailed from Norway. | |
| 5 | **ICE DAMAGE** One destroyer hit by a freak wave and growlers. Severe structural damage. All Radar and Asdic half guns out of action until harbour repair. Speed reduced to maximum of 25 knots. Can be detached and referred to the EBC chart | Resolve |
| 6 | **FIRE.** Deck landing accident causes major fire on fleet carrier. Test for damage and control. Must be detached back to Scapa Flow with an appropriate escort. Flying operations no longer possible. | resolve |
| 7 | **Submerged U Boat detected** at periscope depth, bearing red 25 at 900 yds from leading escort of fleet screen. **Weather**. *Extreme cold. Light wind. Visibility 4 nm calm sea. Snow squalls* | combat |
| | **Undetected Submerged U Boat** at periscope depth, bearing GREEN 90 at 500 yds from leading battleship or cruiser. **Weather**. *Extreme cold. Heavy sleet, strong wind. Rough sea. Visibility 750 yds* | combat |
| 8 | **AIR ATTACK.** Aurora illuminates the area in bright artificial daylight. **Weather.** *Extreme cold visibility 6 nm, choppy seas.* Reduce all AA factors by half due to heavy icing. Ships with radar 285 may engage outside visibility **Roll on AAT 2.** Raid is detected at maximum radar range. If a carrier is present a 3 plane CAP is already in the air and a further three plan flight can be launched before the attack arrives | combat |
| 0 | **RADAR CONTACT** at 18nm, bearing red 40 from leading battleship or cruiser. Roll on ISB 1 for contact and investigate. **Weather**. *Extreme cold. Light wind. Visibility 4 nm calm sea. Snow falls* | Resolve |
| D10 | WINTER HOME FLEET EVENTS BOX    ARCTIC NIGHT | ACTION |
| 1-6 | No enemy contact. Formation proceeds. | Proceed |
| 7 | **ICE DAMAGE.** One cruiser has collided with a growler. Serious flooding. Speed reduced to 20 knots maximum | Resolve |
| 8 | **Submerged U Boat** detected on ASDIC at *periscope* 900yds Red 25 from lead escort on port side. **Weather**. *Extreme cold. Light wind. Visibility 1 nm calm sea. Snow squalls.* | Combat |
| 8 | **Submerged undetected U Boat** bearing Red 50 from lead battleship or cruiser. **Weather** *Heavy seas, high winds. Visibility 500yds, frequent sleet.* Radar range reduced by half due to sea returns and sleet clutter. ASDIC/SONAR factors reduced by one | Combat |
| 9-0 | **INVESTIGATE A SIGHTING.** Radar contact at maximum range from leading ship. **Roll on ISB1**. **Weather** *slight seas, light winds. Visibility 5000yds* | Resolve |

## HOME FLEET WINTER TASK FORCES 1942

- **CF A** = HMS London, HMS Norfolk, HMS Belfast
- **CF B** = HMS Edinburgh, HMS Liverpool, HMS Glasgow, HMS Diomede
- **CF C** = USS Tuscaloosa, USS Augusta, USS Brooklyn, USS Wichita
- **HFB** = HMS Howe, USS Washington (Early 1942), HMS Furious, HMS Bermuda, 1 Tribal class DD, 2 M class DD, 2 Q class DD
- **HFA** = HMS King George V, HMS Anson, HMS Victorious, HMS Berwick, HMS Jamaica, 4 M class DD, 4 A to I class DD

## HOME FLEET WINTER TASK FORCES 1943

- **CF A** = HMS London, HMS Norfolk, HMS Belfast
- **CF B** = HMS Devonshire, HMS Gambia, HMS Liverpool, HMS Diomede
- **CF C** = HMS Mauritius, USS Tuscaloosa, HMS Bermuda, HMS Hawkins, 2 S class DD, 2 M class DD
- **HFB** = HMS Howe, USS Alabama (early-Mid 1943), HMS Furious, HMS Glasgow, 1 Tribal class DD, 2 M class DD, 2 Q class DD, 4 Hunt II
- **HFA** = HMS Anson, HMS Victorious, HMS Berwick, HMS Jamaica, 2 Q class DD, 4 S class DD, 2 R class DD

## HOME FLEET WINTER TASK FORCES 1944 - 1945

- **CF A** = HMS London, HMS Belfast
- **CF B** = HMS Edinburgh, HMS Liverpool, HMS Frobisher, 4 Hunt II
- **CF C** = HMS Norfolk, HMS Glasgow, 1 Battle class DD, 2 Ca Class DD
- **HFB** = HMS Howe, HMS Furious, HMS Formidable (1944), HMS Bermuda, HMS Quilliam, 6 W class DD, 4 Z class DD
- **HFA** = HMS Indefatigable (1944), HMS Victorious (1944), HMS Berwick, HMS Jamaica, 6 V class DD, 1 Tribal class
- **HOME FLEET Escort carriers 1944-45.** Campania, Emperor, Fencer, Nairana, Nabob, Premier, Pursuer, Puncher, Queen, Searcher, Striker, Trumpeter **Battleships** HMS King George V, HMS Anson only until the sinking of the Tirpitz

## HOME FLEET WINTER AIR STRIKES 1942

- **STRIKE X** = 6 Swordfish bombers + 4 Fulmar fighters with a light bomb each
- **STRIKE Y** = 8 Albacore torpedo bombers + 5 Fulmar fighters with a light bomb each
- **STRIKE Z** = 9 Albacore torpedo bombers + 4 Albacore with a heavy bomb each + 8 Sea Hurricane fighters

## HOME FLEET WINTER AIR STRIKES 1943 *(After October use Barracuda instead of Swordfish and Albacore)*

- **STRIKE X.** 6 Swordfish torpedo bombers + 4 Albacore with a heavy bomb each + 4 Martlet
- **STRIKE Y.** 6 Swordfish torpedo bombers + 6 Swordfish with two medium bombs each + 6 Martlet
- **STRIKE Z.** 8 Swordfish torpedo bombers + 6 Albacore bombers with a medium bomb each + 6 Seafire
- **September / October alternative** Use USN Avenger, Dauntless and Wildcat and increase each raid by two aircraft

## HOME FLEET WINTER AIR STRIKES 1944-45

- **STRIKE X.** 8 Barracuda torpedo bombers + 4 Barracuda with one heavy bomb each + 6 Corsair with one medium bomb each
- **STRIKE Y.** 12 Barracuda torpedo bombers + 6 Firefly with a medium bomb each + 6 Corsair with a medium bomb each
- **STRIKE Z.** 12 Barracuda torpedo bombers + 8 Firefly with a medium bomb each + 6 Corsair with one medium bomb each

## SOVIET WINTER ADDITIONAL ESCORTS JOINING CONVOY 1942

- SEG 1. Coast patrol ship Zhemchug. (NKVD manned modified Tral type)
- SEG 2. Old destroyers Uritzky  SEG 3. Old destroyer Karl Lieberknech
- SEG 4. Sokrushitelny, (modern type VII destroyers)
- SEG 5. Grozny, (modern type VII destroyers)
- SEG 6. Gromkiy, Razumny. Stremitelny (modern type VII destroyers)

## SOVIET WINTER ADDITIONAL ESCORTS JOINING CONVOY 1943

- SEG 1. Coast patrol ships Zhemchug and Saffir. (NKVD manned, modified Tral type) Fedor Lidtke Patrol icebreaker
- SEG 2. Old destroyers Artem, Uritzky
- SEG 3. Old destroyers Kuibishev, Karl Lieberknecht
- SEG 4. Razyaryonny, Sokrushitelny, (modern type VII destroyers)
- SEG 5. Grozny, Razyaryonny, Gremyashchy, (modern type VII destroyers)
- SEG 6. Baku, (Leningrad class leader) Gromkiy, Razumny. Stremitelny (modern type VII destroyers)

## SOVIET WINTER ADDITIONAL ESCORTS JOINING CONVOY 1944-45

- SEG 1. Coast patrol ships Zhemchug and Saffir. (NKVD manned, modified Tral type) Fedor Lidtke Patrol icebreaker
- SEG 2. Old destroyers Artem, Uritzky
- SEG 3. Old destroyers Kuibishev, Karl Lieberknecht
- SEG 4. Razyaryonny, Sokrushitelny, (modern type VII destroyers)
- SEG 5. Grozny, Razyaryonny, Gremyashchy, (modern type VII destroyers)
- SEG 6. Baku, (Leningrad class leader) Gromkiy, Razumny. Stremitelny (modern type VII destroyers)

## AIR ATTACK TABLE ONE (Long range)

| D10 | Direction | Aircraft in the attack | Type of attack | Attack load per aircraft |
|---|---|---|---|---|
| 1 | RED 170 | 3 He115 Seaplanes + 1 He115 scout | Low level bombing | 2 Medium |
| 2 | RED 120 | 3 Fw200 Condor + 1 Condor scout | Low level bombing | 4 Light |
| 3 | RED 100 | 4 He115 Seaplanes + 1 He115 scout | Torpedo attack (Low level) | 1 torpedo each |
| 4 | RED 45 | 2 Ju 88 + 1 Ju88 scout | Dive bombing | 1 Medium |
| 5 | RED 15 | 3 Fw200 Condor +1 Condor scout | Low level bombing | 4 Light |
| 6 | GREEN 170 | 3 He115 Seaplanes +1 Condor scout | Low level bombing | 2 Medium per He115 |
| 7 | GREEN 100 | 4 Ju 88 + 1 Ju88 scout | Dive bombing | 1 Medium |
| 8 | GREEN 120 | 4 He115 Seaplanes + 1 He115 scout | Torpedo attack (Low level) | 1 torpedo each |
| 9 | GREEN 90 | 6 Ju 88 + 1 Ju88 scout | Medium level bombing | 4 Light |
| 0 | GREEN 45 | 5 Do21 + 1 Ju88 scout | High level bombing | 4 Light |

## AIR ATTACK TABLE TWO (Medium range)

| D10 | Direction | Aircraft in the attack | Type of attack | Attack load per aircraft |
|---|---|---|---|---|
| 1 | RED 170 | 6 Ju 88 | Dive bombing | 1 Medium |
| 2 | RED 120 | 6 Do17+ 2 Ju88 fighters | High level bombing | 2 Medium (bombers only) |
| 3 | RED 100 | 6 Heinkel III  1 Ju88 scout | Torpedo attack | 1 torpedo |
| 4 | RED 45 | 6 Ju 88 + 2 Ju88 fighters | Low level bombing | 2 Medium (bombers only) |
| 5 | RED 15 | 6 Heinkel III  4 Ju188 fighters | Low level bombing | 2 Medium |
| 6 | GREEN 170 | 6 Ju 88 + 1 Ju88 scout | Dive bombing | 1 Medium |
| 7 | GREEN 100 | 6 Do17+ 2 Ju88 fighters1 Ju88 scout | High level bombing | 2 Medium |
| 8 | GREEN 120 | 6 Heinkel III  1 Fw200 scout | Torpedo attack | 1 torpedo |
| 9 | GREEN 90 | 6 Ju 88 + 4 Ju88 fighters1 Ju88 scout | Low level bombing | 2 Medium (bombers only) |

## AIR ATTACK TABLE THREE (CLOSE range)

| D10 | Direction | Aircraft in the attack | Type of attack | Attack load per aircraft |
|---|---|---|---|---|
| 1 | RED 170 | 9 Ju 87 Stuka + 5 Me110 fighters | Dive bombing | 1 Heavy |
| 2 | RED 120 | 9 Ju 88 + 5 Me110 fighters | Dive bombing | 2 Medium (bombers only) |
| 3 | RED 100 | 9 Do217 + 5 Me110 fighters | Medium level bombing | 4 Medium (bombers only) |
| 4 | Multidirectional | 9 Ju88 + 5 Me110 fighters | Torpedo attack (Low level) | 1 Torpedo |
| 5 | GREEN 45 | 9 Heinkel III + 3 Ju88 fighters | Golden comb torpedo attack | 2 Torpedoes (Low level) |
| 6 | GREEN 170 | 9 Ju 87 Stuka + 5 Me110 fighters | Dive bombing | 1 Heavy |
| 7 | GREEN 100 | 9 Ju 88 + 5 Me110 fighters | Dive bombing | 2 Medium (bombers only) |
| 8 | GREEN 120 | 9 He111 + 5 Me110 fighters | Low level bombing | 2 Medium (bombers only) |
| 9 | Multidirectional | 9 Ju88 + 5 Me110 fighters | Torpedo attack (Low level) | 1 Torpedo |
| 0 | GREEN 45 | 9 Heinkel III + 3 Ju188 fighters | Golden comb torpedo attack | 2 torpedoes (Low level) |

## AIR ATTACK TABLE FOUR (Short range)

| D10 | Direction | Aircraft in the attack | Type of attack | Attack load per aircraft |
|---|---|---|---|---|
| 1 | RED 170 | 12 Ju 87 Stuka + 6 Me110 fighters | Dive bombing | 1 Heavy |
| 2 | Multidirectional | 12 Ju 88 + 6 Me210 fighters | Dive bombing | 1 Heavy (bombers only) |
| 3 | Multidirectional | 12 He111 + 6 Me109 fighters | High level bombing | 2 Medium (bombers only) |
| 4 | RED 15 | 12 Heinkel III + 6 Ju188 fighters | High level bombing | 2 Medium (bombers only) |
| 5 | RED 45 | 12 Heinkel III + 6 Ju88 + 6 Fw190 Fighters | High level bombing | 2 Medium (bombers only) |
| 6 | GREEN 170 | 12 Ju 87 Stuka + 5 Me110 fighters | Dive bombing | 1 Heavy |
| 7 | Multidirectional | 12 Ju 88 + 6 Me110 fighters | Dive bombing | 2 Medium (bombers only) |
| 8 | Multidirectional | 12 He111 + 6 Me110 fighters | Medium level bombing | 2 Medium (bombers only) |
| 9 | RED 15 | 12 Heinkel III + 6 Ju188 fighters | Medium level bombing | 2 Medium (bombers only) |
| 0 | RED 45 | 12 Ju 87 Stuka + 8 Me110 fighters | Dive bombing | 1 Heavy (Stukas only) |

### AIR ATTACK SPECIAL NOTE
Air attacks assisted by a scout to drop flares do not count as low level on detection because the scout must fly at medium to high.

### ⭐ SOVIET OR ALLIED AIR COVER TABLE (Short range) 1941

| D10 | Position | Number | Type of aircraft | Nationality |
|---|---|---|---|---|
| 1-5 | | | No air cover available | |
| 6 | 3nm ahead | 4 | Hurricane IIB | British |
| 7 | 5nm ahead | 3 | I-16 or I152 | Soviet |
| 8 | overhead | 3 | MiG-3 | Soviet |
| 9 | 3nm starboard | 3 | Yak-1 | Soviet |
| 0 | 2nm astern | 4 | LaGG-3 | Soviet |

### ⭐ SOVIET OR ALLIED AIR COVER TABLE (Short range) 1942

| D10 | Position | Number | Type of aircraft | Nationality |
|---|---|---|---|---|
| 1-4 | | | No air cover available | |
| 5 | 4nm Ahead | 4 | Hurricane IIB | British |
| 6 | 3nm astern | 4 | P-40C | Soviet |
| 7 | 4nm starboard | 4 | Yak-3 | Soviet |
| 8 | 3nm ahead | 4 | LaGG-3 | Soviet |
| 9 | 5nm ahead | 3 | Yak1 | Soviet |
| 0 | overhead | 4 | MiG3 | Soviet |

### ⭐ SOVIET OR ALLIED AIR COVER TABLE (Short range) 1943

| D10 | Position | Number | Type of aircraft | Nationality |
|---|---|---|---|---|
| 1-3 | | | No air cover available | |
| 4 | 4nm starboard | 4 | Hurricane IIB | Soviet |
| 5 | 5nm ahead | 4 | P-39 | Soviet |
| 6 | 3nm port | 4 | P-40E | Soviet |
| 7-8 | overhead | 5 | Yak-7 | Soviet |
| 9-0 | 5nm astern | 5 | LaGG-3 | Soviet |

### ⭐ SOVIET OR ALLIED AIR COVER TABLE (Short range) 1944-45

| D10 | Position | Number | Type of aircraft | Nationality |
|---|---|---|---|---|
| 1-2 | | | No air cover available | |
| 3 | overhead | 4 | Hurricane IIB | Soviet |
| 4 | overhead | 4 | P-40E | Soviet |
| 5 | 3nm astern | 4 | P39 | Soviet |
| 6 | 3nm ahead | 6 | P47 | Soviet |
| 7 | 3nm starboard | 6 | P-40C | Soviet |
| 8 | 4nm port | 6 | Yak-7 | Soviet |
| 9-0 | 3nm ahead | 6 | Yak-9 | Soviet |

### ⭐ SOVIET OR ALLIED AIR COVER TABLE L (Long range) 1942-45

| D10 | Position | Number | Type of aircraft | Nationality |
|---|---|---|---|---|
| 1-6 | | | No air cover available | |
| 7 | overhead | 2 | Pe-2 | Soviet |
| 8 | 5nm astern | 3 | Pe-2 | Soviet |
| 9-0 | 5nm ahead | 4 | Pe-3 | Soviet |

The air cover table shows the location of the air cover in relation to the convoy plus the number and type at the time an enemy air attack is detected.

# EVENTS BEYOND THE CONVOY CHART

| ROMPER | STRAGGLER | DAMAGED OR BROKEN DOWN SHIP WITH AN ESCORT | DAMAGED SHIP | MERCHANT CREW ABANDONED SHIP |
|---|---|---|---|---|
| Move ship to Holding Area leaves the tactical zone proceeding as independent ahead of convoy at a faster speed. | Move ship to holding area. No longer in touch with or unable to keep convoy speed | A damaged ship under tow can have an escort provided to give ASW protection. However that ship must not tow or assist with the tow | Move ship to holding area. No longer in touch with, and unable to maintain the convoy speed | Move ship to holding area. Left behind and no longer in touch with the convoy |
| **If a WOLFPACK or more than ten aircraft attacked the convoy after the ship became a straggler roll D10** | **If a WOLFPACK attacked the convoy after the ship became a straggler roll D10** | **If a WOLFPACK or more than 10 aircraft attacked the convoy after the ship became a straggler roll D10** | Crew will abandon ship if struck by a torpedo which causes 50% damage, causes critical flooding or a major fire | **ROLL D10** |
| 1= Ship boarded by Germans and valuable documents seized. Ship then finished off by them. Crew POW victory pts x 2 | 1 =Ship boarded by Germans and valuable documents seized. Ship then finished off by them. Crew POW victory points x2 | 1 = Sunk but crew rescued Points to Germans | If so refer right to the abandoned ship column | 1-4= Finished off by U Boat Points to German player |
| 2- 4 = Sunk with all hands. Points to Germans | 2- 6 = Sunk with all hands. Points to Germans | 2 = Two Torpedoes fired at it from optimum angle at range 6000yds Test for hits and damage. Points to Germans if sunk | If a rescue ship is present or rescue designated trawler, the crew are able to be rescued as per rules for rescue | 5-6= Finished off by German Aircraft Pts to German player |
| 5 = Two Torpedoes fired at it from optimum angle at range 4000yds Test for hits and damage. Germans pts if sunk | 7-8 = Returns independently to its port of departure. No points to either side | 3-4 = Ship beached on friendly shore 1/2 pts to Germans | | 7=Sunk by allied warships to prevent hazard to shipping |
| 6= Ship beached on friendly coast. Half points value gained by Axis | 9= Ship beached on friendly shore. Half points value gained by Germans | 5-8= Reaches intended port with cargo damage. ½ pts to Allies | SOE can provide a ship to tow or a tow plus escort. If tow move right two to the straggler column. If tow and escort move right to the damaged ship with escort column | 8=Ship boarded by enemy, valuable documents seized. Ship then finished off Double victory points to Germans |
| 7-0 = Reaches intended port independently full points | 0= Reached intended port full points value to Allies | 9-0= Reaches intended port full points value to by Allies | | 9=Sunk by allied aircraft to avoid capture |
| **If NO Wolfpack attacks occurred or attacks by ten or more aircraft, after ship became a romper Roll D10** | **If N0 Wolfpack attacks occurred after the ship became a straggler Roll D10** | **If NO Wolfpack or 10 or less aircraft attacked convoy after separation Roll D10** | NOTE Virtually all merchant ships came to a halt after being hit with a torpedo to avoid further damage from sea and collapsing bulkheads. They can resume movement after two combat moves. If able to catch up to the convoy the rejoin | |
| 1 = Sunk by U Boat, with all hands Points to Germans | 1- 2 = Sunk with all hands. Points to Axis | 1 = Sunk but crew rescued Points to Axis | | 0= Located by high seas rescue tug and independent Escort. Towed to nearest Allied port. ½ points to Allies |
| 2-3 = Sunk by aircraft. Crew not rescued points to Germans | 3-4 = Sunk crew rescued | 2 = One Torpedo fired at it from optimum at range 6000yds Test for hit and any damage | | |
| 4-5 = Ship beached on Murman coast. ½ pts value to Germans | 5 = | 3 = Ship beached on friendly shore. 1/2 pts to Germans | | |
| 6-7= Returned to port of departure No points to either | 6= Ship beached on Murman coast. ½ pts value to Axis | 4-8 = Reaches intended port with cargo damage. ½ pts to Allies | | |
| 8-0 = Reached Russian port full points to Allies | 7-0= Reached intended port full points value to Allies | 9-0= Towed back to port of origin. No pts to either side | | |

**Many thanks to Lonnie Gill for the idea to provide this chart.**

| | |
|---|---|
| If a straggler or damaged ship rejoins the convoy it is automatically presumed that any engineering damage must have been repaired sufficiently to enable the ship to temporarily rejoin at convoy speed. If it is hit again, original speed loss is re-applied along with any new damage. | **MISSING CODES** The British Admiralty was continually worried about secret papers and especially codes, falling into the hands of the enemy. If a ship is reported missing without trace, add 5 victory points to the German total. If papers were or were not captured, there was still the concern and need to change codes etc just in case. |

| D10 | SUMMER NORTHERN NIGHT NE1 | Result |
|---|---|---|
| 1-8 | **No enemy contact.** Convoy proceeds | Resolve |
| 9 | **MINES.** Convoy sails into drifting mines. Roll 1-2 = no ships struck. 3-6 = one merchant struck hit. 7-8 two merchant struck 9 = one destroyer of fighting escort struck. 0 = Larger warship of fighting escort struck | Resolve |
| 0 | **Panic.** One merchant ship panics, and fires a snowflake illuminant rocket to starboard of convoy. **Axis player** may attack with 1 surfaced submarine of choice from 4,000 yds and starboard bearing of choice against any visible illuminated ship of the close escort. **WEATHER** sleet rain, rough sea, strong wind from NE, visibility 500yds but illuminated range 6000 yds. | Combat |
|  | **SUMMER NORTHERN NIGHT NE-2** | Result |
| 1-6 | **No enemy contact.** Convoy proceeds | Resolve |
| 7-8 | **German U Boat submerged** on bearing RED 90, 750yds from lead ship of column one. Allies test for detection. **WEATHER.** Aurora illuminates the area in artificial daylight. Visibility 5nm. Seas slight. Slight wind from NE. Intense cold | Combat |
| 9 | **Undetected U boat submerged** bearing RED 90, 450yds from second ship of column one. **WEATHER** heavy sleet, choppy sea and high winds from NNE. Visibility 500yds. Test for detection. All gunnery and ASW factors reduced by half due to icing | Combat |
| 0 | **German U Boat** submerged. Detected on bearing red 45, 1500yds from the leading portside close escort of convoy. **WEATHER.** Aurora illuminates the area in artificial daylight. Visibility 7nm. Seas choppy. Slight wind fro NE. Intense cold | Combat |

| D10 | DE-1  ARCTIC SUMMER DAYLIGHT EVENTS 1 | Result |
|---|---|---|
| 1-2 | **No enemy contact.** Convoy proceeds **British Catalina** will support convoy next daylight move. Decide placement now. | Proceed |
| 3 | German Fw200 made a brief contact with convoy but was unable to be intercepted. Add 2 to die roll for next night move | Proceed |
| 4 | **SMOKEY JOE,** one merchant ship is making excessive smoke. Add 3 to die roll for next night move **British Catalina** will support convoy next daylight move. Decide placement now. | Resolve |
| 5 | **MINE.** One merchant ship has set off two floating mines. Roll as 2 torpedo hits. **WEATHER** Clear sky, Visibility 9nm Seas choppy | Resolve |
| 6 | **ENEMY AIRCRAFT.** Fw200 Condor circles convoy for one hour, out of gun range, while transmitting details to its base. If **CAM ship** present it can launch. If **CVE** present a two aircraft fighter CAP can engage Condor. If not driven off and add 4 to the die roll for next night move **WEATHER** Clear sky, Visibility 10nm choppy seas | Resolve |
| 0 | **U Boat** Undetected submerged in firing position, bearing RED 45 at Range 3,000 yds from the lead ship, column 4. **WEATHER** rough sea, high winds from NNE and rainsqualls, visibility 5nm. | Combat |

| | DE 2  ARCTIC SUMMER DAYLIGHT EVENTS BOX 2 | |
|---|---|---|
| 1-7 | **No enemy contact.** Convoy proceeds **British Wellington** will support convoy next move. Decide placement now. **If a night move aircraft is equipped with Leigh Light** | Resolve |
| 8 | **SMOKEY JOE.** One ship making excessive smoke. Add 3 to die roll for next night move **British Wellington** will support convoy next move. Decide placement now. **If a night move aircraft is equipped with Leigh Light** | Resolve |
| 9 | **Air attack.** 3 Do217 with two Fritz X missiles each, Bearing GREEN 135, from lead starboard close escort **at** range 10nm miles. German player decides targets. **Too rough to launch aircraft. WEATHER** heavy seas. Visibility 7nm. high winds from NNW | Combat |
| 0 | German U Boat at periscope depth, bearing GREEN 10, 3000 yds from leading ship of fighting escort. Allies test for detection. **HF/DF report** U Boat sending sighting report but beyond ground wave. Add one to die roll for next night move | Combat |

| | DE 3  ARCTIC SUMMER DAYLIGHT EVENTS BOX 3 | |
|---|---|---|
| 1-7 | **No enemy contact.** Merchant ships join the convoy from Reykjavik. Convoy proceeds **2 British Wellingtons** will support convoy next move. Decide placement now. **If a night move aircraft are equipped with Leigh Light** | Proceed |
| 8 | German Ju290 made a brief contact with convoy. Add 2 to die roll for next night move. Merchant ships join the convoy from Reykjavik **MINE** One merchant ship has struck a mine. **Weather** heavy seas, rainstorms, too rough to launch aircraft | Proceed |
| 9-0 | If CVE present, ASW aircraft has surprised a German U Boat diving on bearing RED ten from lead escort at range 7 nm. If no CVE present, the detecting aircraft is a USAAF Catalina. **Attack carried out while U Boat still diving to shallow.** Merchant ships join the convoy from Reykjavik, approaching from GREEN 90. **WEATHER** moderate seas visibility 12nm | Combat |

| | DE 4  ARCTIC SUMMER DAYLIGHT EVENTS BOX 4 | |
|---|---|---|
| 1-3 | **No enemy contact British Wellington** will support convoy next move. Decide placement now. **If a night move aircraft is equipped with Leigh Light** | Proceed |
| 4 | **BREAKDOWN** One escort is suffering s machinery problem is detached to Seidisfjord and will be unable to rejoin. **USAAF Catalina** will support convoy next move. Decide placement now | Resolve |
| 5 | **A MAJOR** fire has broken out on board one merchant ship. If damage is too severe, it can be detached to Reykjavik. | Resolve |
| 6 | German U Boat at periscope depth undetected on bearing RED 30 Range 2500yds from rear merchant ship of port column. **WEATHER** low cloud visibility 5nm choppy seas and heavy rain squalls strong wing from NNE | Combat |
| 8 | **Multiple HF/DF bearings** red 45 from ship 1 column 1. A U Boat is on the surface within ground wave sending contact report. **If you do not investigate**, add 3 to die rolls next NIGHT campaign phase. Weather Visibility 5nm Sea state rough strong wind from NNE | ISB3 |
| 9-0 | **Unknown object** bearing red 45, range 8 miles from starboard close escort **Weather** Visibility 12nm choppy seas strong wind from NE | ISB2 |

| | DE5 ARCTIC SUMMER DAYLIGHT EVENTS BOX 5 | |
|---|---|---|
| 1-4 | **No enemy contact**. Convoy proceeds. **REFUELING** not possible this move. Two destroyers must refuel by dawn of day 7 or detach to Seidisfjord to refuel. Rejoin on dawn of day 8. Two **USAAF Catalina's** will support convoy next move. Decide placement now | Resolve |
| 5 | **German Fw200** detected by radar, in contact with convoy at long range. If a **CVE** is present, two fighters can engage. Add 3 to die roll for next night move if it is not shot down. **Weather** Visibility 12 nm Sea state choppy **REFUELING may be carried out** | Combat |
| 6 | **German Ju290** in radar contact with convoy at long range. If **CVE** present, one fighter can engage. Add 3 to die roll for next night move if it is not shot down **REFUELING may be carried out. Weather** Fog banks. Visibility 2 nm Sea state slight. Extreme cold. | Resolve |
| 7 | **WEATHER**. Severe storm, very heavy seas, visibility 2nm. **REFUELING** not possible One merchant ship damaged by heavy seas and cargo shift. Test for critical flooding Two **RAF Hudson aircraft** will support convoy next move. Decide placement now | Resolve |
| 8 | **Undetected, submerged U Boat** bearing green 45, range 1,600yds from leading escort starboard side, has fired two torpedoes at it. Axis player selects which submarine to use. **WEATHER** rain squalls, visibility 2nm, choppy seas **REFUELING may be carried out.** RAF Sunderland aircraft available next move. **Allocate patrol position now.** | Combat |
| 9 | **GROWLERS**. Convoy encounters floating ice pack. *Speed* of all ships reduced to 5 knots. One Escort loses ASDIC/Sonar due to ice damage. **AIR ATTACK**. Roll on Air Attack table 1. Raid detected at maximum radar range. **CVE** is unable to launch due to speed restriction. **CAM Ship** may launch for intercept at long range. *WEATHER*. Extreme cold. Light wind. Visibility 8 nm calm seas. **REFUELING** may be carried out. Two **RAF Hudson aircraft** will support convoy next move. Decide placement now | Combat |
| 0 | **AIR ATTACK**. If German aircraft in contact with convoy in any previous move roll on Air Attack Table 1. If a **CVE** is present, two fighters can engage raid at 10nm. Two more can engage raid at 5nm. **CAM Ship** may launch in time for intercept at 5nm. *WEATHER*. Extreme cold. Light wind. Visibility 7 nm calm seas. **REFUELING may be carried out** | Resolve |
| **D10** | **DE6 ARCTIC SUMMER DAYLIGHT EVENTS BOX 6** | |
| 1-5 | **No enemy contact. REFUELING may be carried out. *WEATHER* Extreme cold. Snow squalls. Visibility 2 nm choppy seas.** | Proceed |
| 6-7 | **GROWLERS**. Convoy encounters heavy floating ice pack. *Speed* of all ships reduced to 5 knots. One Escort suffers ASDIC/Sonar breakdown due to ice. Unable to repair. **AIR ATTACK**. Roll on Air Attack table 2. High or medium Raid detected at maximum radar range. Low level detected at maximum visibility. CAM ship may launch for intercept at 6nm. **Carrier** is unable to launch due to speed restriction. **NO REFUELING** may be carried out. *WEATHER* Extreme cold. Heavy rainsqualls. Visibility 3 nm heavy seas. **Two destroyers of the fighting escort are in need of fuel. Must detach to Seidisfjord and rejoin at start of second move of day 7** | Resolve |
| 8 | **HEAVY STORM**. No further event rolls this day. **Proceed straight to twilight events** One merchant ship has become a straggler. Refer to EBC table. *WEATHER* heavy seas. Heavy rain visibility 3nm | Proceed |
| 9 | **SEVERE STORM**. No further event rolls this day. **Proceed straight to twilight events** One merchant ship has suffered a cargo shift. Major flooding Two merchant ships have become stragglers. Refer to EBC table. Escorts in need of fuel may detach to Bell Sound and rejoin for the last day move of day 13. *WEATHER* extreme seas sleet squalls visibility 2nm | Proceed |
| 0 | **SEVERE STORM**. No further event rolls this day. **Proceed straight to first move of day 7**. Three merchant ships and two escorts have become stragglers. Refer to EBC table. Escorts in need of fuel cannot detach to Seidisfjord because conditions are too severe. *WEATHER* extreme seas. Heavy sleet and snow squalls visibility 1nm Full gale from NE. **NO REFUELING** may be carried out. | Proceed |
| | **DE7 ARCTIC SUMMER DAYLIGHT EVENTS BOX 7** | |
| 1-4 | **No enemy contact** convoy proceeds **REFUELING may be carried out.** | Proceed |
| 5-6 | **Undetected, submerged U Boat** bearing green 10, range 6000yds from leading escort. **NO REFUELING** may be carried out. *WEATHER* Extreme cold. Rain squalls. Visibility 6nm choppy seas strong wind from NNE. **Two destroyers require refuelling during next day** | Combat |
| 7-8 | **AIR ATTACK**. Roll on air attack table 3. Carrier or CAM ship may not launch due to severe icing from frozen sea spray. Reduce all AA factors by half due to icing **Surfaced U Boat** bearing dead ahead range 7nm from leading ship of fighting escort. *WEATHER Extreme cold sleet squalls. Visibility 6nm choppy seas Fresh gale from NNW.* **NO REFUELING** may be carried out. | Combat |
| 9 | **AIR ATTACK**. Roll on air attack table 3 twice for **separate raids one hour apart.** If Carrier present it may intercept raids at 7nm with 3 aircraft. **CAM ship may launch** to intercept raid at 5nm *WEATHER Extreme cold. Rain squalls. Fresh gale from NNW. Visibility 6nm rough seas* **NO REFUELING** may be carried out. | Combat |
| 0 | **AIR ATTACK**. Roll on air attack table 3 three times for **separate raids one hour apart.** If Carrier present it may intercept raids at 7nm with 3 aircraft. **CAM ship may launch** to intercept raid at 5nm *WEATHER Extreme cold. Rain squalls. Fresh gale from NNW. Visibility 6nm heavy seas* **NO REFUELING** may be carried out. | Combat |
| | **DE8 ARCTIC SUMMER DAYLIGHT EVENTS BOX 8** | |
| 1-4 | **No enemy contact** convoy proceed. **Fighting escort Destroyers must be detached to Bell Sound for fuel. Will rejoin convoy** on twilight move of day 11. **If cruiser** in fighting escort it will remain with convoy. | Proceed |
| 5-6 | **AIR ATTACK**. Roll on air attack table 3. If Carrier present it may intercept raid at 10nm with CAP. **CAM ship may launch** to intercept raid at 5nm *WEATHER Extreme cold clear day. Visibility 20 nm mild seas* | Combat |
| 7-8 | **AIR ATTACK**. Roll on air attack table 3 twice for **separate raids one hour apart.** If Carrier present it may intercept raids at 10nm with CAP. **CAM ship may launch** to intercept raid at 5nm *WEATHER Extreme cold clear day. Visibility 20 nm mild seas* | Combat |
| 9 | **AIR ATTACK**. Roll on air attack table 3 three times for **separate raids one hour apart.** If Carrier present it may intercept raids at 10nm with 2 aircraft. **CAM ship may launch** to intercept raid at 5nm *WEATHER Extreme cold Visibility 10 nm mild seas* | Combat |
| 0 | **Two British Hunt II destroyers** join close escort from Bell Sound. Approach from Red 90 sighted at 5nm. **Submerged U Boat** bearing green 120, 5000yds from rear escort on the starboard side of convoy. *WEATHER Extreme cold Visibility 10 nm mild seas* | Combat |

| | DE9 ARCTIC SUMMER DAYLIGHT EVENTS BOX 9 | |
|---|---|---|
| 1-5 | **No enemy contact** convoy proceed. | Proceed |
| 6 | **AIR ATTACK. Roll on air attack table 2. WEATHER** Extreme cold. Visibility 10 nm very rough sea. Strong wind gusts from North. **Carrier unable to launch** | Combat |
| 7 | **AIR ATTACK. Roll on air attack table 3. If Carrier** present it may intercept raid at 5nm if CAP available. . **CAM ship may launch** to intercept raid at 5nm **WEATHER** Extreme cold clear day. Visibility 20 nm mild seas Light SE breeze | Combat |
| 8 | **AIR ATTACK. Roll on air attack table 3 twice for separate raids one hour apart. If Carrier** present it may intercept both raids at 10nm if CAP available. **CAM ship may launch** to intercept raid at 5nm. **U Boat mistakenly surfaces** on bearing red 30 range 6000yds from port ship of fighting escort. **WEATHER** Extreme cold clear day. Visibility 20 nm mild seas Light SE breeze | Combat |
| 9 | **AIR ATTACK. Roll on air attack table 3 three times for separate raids one hour apart. If Carrier** present it may intercept raid at 10nm if CAP available. **CAM ship may launch** to intercept raid at 5nm **WEATHER** Mild. Visibility 10 nm mild sea. Light SE breeze | Combat |
| 0 | **AIR ATTACK. Roll on air attack table 3 twice for separate raids one hour apart and +2 to D19. If Carrier** present it may only intercept the first raid at 10nm with CAP. Landing accidents prevent CAP being renewed for second raid. **CAM ship may launch** to intercept raid at 5nm **Undetected submerged U Boat** bearing green 10 range 8000yds from leading close escort. **WEATHER** Mild. Visibility 10 nm mild sea. Light SE breeze | Combat |
| **D10** | **DE10 ARCTIC SUMMER DAYLIGHT EVENTS BOX 10** | Action |
| 1-4 | **No enemy contact** convoy proceeds | Proceed |
| 5-6 | **AIR ATTACK. Roll on air attack table 4 and then 3 for separate raids one hour apart. If Carrier** present it may intercept both raids at 10nm if CAP available. **CAM ship may launch** to intercept raid at 5nm **WEATHER** cold clear day. Visibility 20 nm mild seas Light SE breeze | Combat |
| 7 | **AIR ATTACK. Roll twice on air attack table 4 for separate raids two hours apart. If Carrier** present it may intercept both raids at 15nm if CAP available. **CAM ship may launch** to intercept raid at 10nm **Undetected submerged U Boat** bearing red 45, range 2000yds from leading ship of column 3 **WEATHER** cold hazy day. Visibility 7 nm choppy seas strong SE wind | |
| 0-8 | **Surface contact** bearing GREEN 45 15 miles from lead ship of the fighting escort, Summer enemy contact chart. **WEATHER** Extreme cold very clear day. Visibility 20 nm mild seas | ISB-1 |
| | **DE11 ARCTIC SUMMER DAYLIGHT EVENTS BOX 11** | |
| 1-4 | **No enemy contact** convoy proceeds | Proceed |
| 5 | **Mines.** One merchant ship and one escort strike mines. **Undetected submerged U Boat** bearing green 45, range 2000yds from rear ship of the port column of convoy | Resolve |
| 5-8 | **AIR ATTACK. Roll on air attack table 3. Carrier may not launch** due to any wind. **WEATHER** Mild day. Visibility 12nm smooth seas no wind. **Roll on Soviet or Allied Air Cover Table** for close air support. | Resolve |
| 9 | **AIR ATTACK. Roll on air attack table 3 twice for separate raids one hour apart. If Carrier** present it may intercept raids at 7nm with 3 aircraft. **CAM ship may launch** to intercept raid at 5nm **Roll on Soviet or Allied Air Cover Table** for close air support. **WEATHER** warm clear day. Visibility 20 nm mild seas slight wind from SSE | Resolve |
| 0 | **Surface contact** bearing 10 miles dead ahead of lead ship of the fighting escort, Summer enemy contact chart. **WEATHER** cold clear day. Visibility 20 nm mild seas slight wind from SW | ISB-2 |
| | **DE12 ARCTIC SUMMER DAYLIGHT EVENTS BOX 12** | |
| 1-5 | **No enemy contact** convoy proceeds. **Fighting Escort detach and proceed to Kola to refuel and return to Iceland** | Proceed |
| 8 | **AIR ATTACK. Roll on air attack table 4. If Carrier** present it may intercept raid at 10nm with CAP. **CAM ship may launch** to intercept raid at 5nm **Roll on Soviet or Allied Air Cover Table** for close air support. **WEATHER** warm clear day. Visibility 20 nm mild seas slight wind from SSE | Resolve |
| 9 | **AIR ATTACK. Roll on air attack table 4 twice for separate raids one hour apart. If Carrier** present it may intercept raids at 10nm with CAP. **CAM ship may launch** to intercept raid at 5nm **WEATHER** Mild. Visibility 10 nm mild sea. Light SE breeze | Resolve |
| 0 | **AIR ATTACK. Roll on air attack table 3 three times for separate raids one hour apart. If Carrier** present it may intercept raids at 10nm with CAP. **CAM ship may launch** to intercept raid at 5nm **WEATHER** Mild. Visibility 10 nm mild sea. Light SE breeze | Resolve |

| D10 | SUMMER EVENTS BOX — Arctic twilight. TwE1 | |
|---|---|---|
| 1-6 | **No enemy contact.** Convoy proceeds in low visibility and choppy seas | Proceed |
| 7 | *HEAVY WEATHER*, low cloud. All further rolls this day **& coming night cancelled.** Proceed to 1st move of next day | Proceed |
| 8 | BREAKDOWN. Merchant Ship has suffered major engineering failure. Detach one escort to tow it back to nearest port | Resolve |
| 9 | BREAKDOWN. One Cruiser or fleet destroyer in the fighting escort has suffered a major engineering failure and must be detached with an escort to return it to base at a maximum of 10 knots. *Weather*. *Visibility 2nm. Seas rough* | Resolve |
| 0 | U BOAT on surface close to convoy, bearing red 90 from leading close escort port side, range 3nm. ALLIES test for detection. *Heavy weather and rough seas. Visibility 2nm. Wind medium from NNE.* **Roll on this event box again** Ships with radar 285 may engage outside visibility | Combat |
| | SUMMER EVENTS BOX — Arctic twilight. TwE2 | |
| 1-7 | **No enemy contact.** Convoy proceeds in low visibility and choppy seas | Proceed |
| 8 | SURPRISE. U Boat on surface visually sighted surfacing on bearing green 145 at range 2500yds from rear ship of the close escort. U Boat also sights the escort. Mutual surprise. German first move. *Weather Very cold. Slight seas light snow. Light NE wind. Visibility 2500 yds* | Combat |
| 9 | U Boat submerged bearing green 90 at range 4000 yds from first ship in the column one. ALLIES test for detection. *Weather choppy seas, sleet, extreme cold, low cloud, strong SE wind, visibility 3nm* | Combat |
| 0 | WEATHER. *Very Heavy seas low cloud and sleet.* Convoy undetected. All further rolls this day **& coming night cancelled.** Proceed to 1st move of next day. **Ships that have suffered floatation damage** roll for a further minor flooding and control | Proceed |
| | SUMMER EVENTS BOX — Arctic twilight. TwE3 | |
| 1-6 | CONVOY Rendezvous point met. Local escort detached and proceed to Seidisfjord. Convoy proceeds with through escort | Proceed |
| 7 | CONVOY Rendezvous point met. If the convoy was previous sighted or attacked by U boats or aircraft, Roll once on **Air Attack** Table 1. Raid fails to find the main convoy and will attack the local escort that detached for Seidisfjord. *Weather Mild seas. Icy cold. Visibility 2nm. Slight NW wind.* High or medium Raid detected at maximum radar range. Low level at 3nm. Ships with radar 285 may engage outside visibility. | Combat |
| 8 | CONVOY Rendezvous point met. Two merchant ships collide. If unable to continue they will proceed to Reykjavik with the departing local escort. *Weather Rough seas. Visibility 4nm.* | Combat |
| 9 | CONVOY Rendezvous missed. Un-detected U Boat submerged in attack position bearing green 40 at range 2000 yds from third ship in the starboard column. Sonar effectiveness of all ships reduced by 1. *Weather Choppy seas. Visibility 4 nm.* **Roll on this event box again until rendezvous met. Roll on next night box twice as convoy is now behind schedule** | Combat |
| 0 | CONVOY Rendezvous met but delayed by severe weather conditions. Local escort detached and proceed to Seidisfjord. Convoy proceeds with through escort. Roll on the next event box (N4) twice instead of once unless cancelled out by previous event roll on TW 2 | Proceed |
| | SUMMER EVENTS BOX — Arctic twilight. TwE4 | |
| 1-4 | GROWLERS. Convoy enters floating ice field. Ships with previous floatation damage suffer automatic minor flooding and roll for control. *Weather Clear, mild seas Light SE wind, Icy cold.* **HOME FLEET.** Roll on the Home Fleet Arctic twilight box **REFUELING** may be carried out | Proceed |
| 5 | WEATHER. Sleet and extreme seas. Gale force winds from NW. Visibility 500yds. All ships stream collision buoys. Test roll 1-5 on D10 for collision between first and second ships of a column. Roll for which. **REFUELING** not possible. | Resolve |
| 6 | WEATHER. Sleet and very heavy seas. Full Gale from NW. Visibility 500yds. One merchant ship damaged by heavy seas and cargo shift. Test for major flooding **REFUELING not possible.** Ships unable to refuel must detach to Seidisfjord and will not return to the convoy. | Resolve |
| 7-8 | Submerged U Boat detected bearing green 10 at range 2000 yds from leading ship of fighting escort. *Weather. Mild seas. Icy cold. Moderate wind from North. Visibility 3nm* Sonar conditions excellent + 1 to all ASDIC and Sonar sets. **ULTRA message from Admiralty.** German warships have sailed from Norway. Die rolls on TW 6 now add +3. **REFUELING** may be carried out | Resolve |
| 9-0 | WEATHER. *Choppy seas low cloud and sleet.* Convoy undetected. All further rolls this day **& coming night cancelled.** Proceed to 1st move of next day. **Ships that have suffered floatation damage** roll for a further minor flooding and control. **REFUELING** may be carried out | Proceed |

| D10 | SUMMER EVENTS BOX    Arctic twilight. TwE5 | |
|---|---|---|
| 1-3 | **No enemy contact.** Convoy proceeds in low visibility, extreme cold and moderate seas **REFUELING** may be carried out | Proceed |
| 4 | **ENGINEERING.** One ship of the fighting escort is suffering condenseritis. Maximum speed reduced to half. Unable to repair at sea **WEATHER.** *Extreme cold and choppy seas.* **REFUELING** may be carried out | Resolve |
| 5 | **SERIOUS FIRE** has broken out on board one merchant ship. **Roll again 2 for this event box at +2** due to visible smoke. **RE-INFORCEMENTS.** SEG 4 joins close escort. **WEATHER.** *Extreme cold and strong swell.* **REFUELING** may be carried out | Resolve |
| 6-7 | **AIR ATTACK. Roll on Air Attack table 2.** High or medium Raid detected at maximum radar range approaching from North. **CAM** ship may launch. **CAP** can intercept outside AA range. **Carrier** launches 3 fighters to intercept inside long AA range. Low level Raid detected at visibility. *Weather clear twilight. Calm seas. Extreme cold. Visibility 6nm.* **HOME FLEET.** Roll on the Home Fleet Arctic twilight box. **REFUELING** may be carried out | Combat |
| 8 | **ULTRA** message from Admiralty. German warships have sailed from Norway. **Die rolls on TW 6 now +3.** One merchant ship becomes a straggler during heavy storm. Test on Events Beyond Convoy table. **REFUELING** not possible. | Proceed |
| 8 | **GROWLERS.** Convoy encounters heavy floating ice pack. **Speed** of all ships reduced to half their normal. One Escort suffers Radar breakdown due to ice. Unable to repair. **AIR ATTACK.** Roll on Air Attack table 3. High or medium Raid detected at maximum radar range approaching from astern. **CAP** may intercept outside AA range. No launch from Carrier due to icing. Low level detected at maximum visibility astern. *Weather. Extreme cold and icing. Light wind from NE. Visibility 4 nm calm seas* All AA factors reduced by half due to icing. **REFUELING** may be carried out | Resolve |
| 0 | **RADAR CONTACT. Unknown ship** bearing green 45, range 12 miles. Fighting escort already deployed in battle formation on contact side of the convoy if admiralty warning previously received. Detach to intercept. *Weather. Visibility 5nm Sea state choppy. Strong wind from NW.* All gunnery and Torpedo factors reduced by half due to icing and conditions. *Roll on ISB2.* **Also roll on HF1 Box** | Resolve |
| | SUMMER EVENTS BOX    Arctic twilight. TwE 6 | |
| 1-4 | **No enemy contact.** Convoy proceeds. SEG 5 joins the close escort. **ULTRA** message from Admiralty. German warships have sailed from Norway. | |
| 5 | **AIR ATTACK.** Roll on Air Attack table 3. *Cloud base low Air attacks at medium must attack from low. Air attacks at high will abort.* Raid detected at maximum radar range. **CAM** ship may launch fighter for intercept at long AA range. Carrier cannot launch due to rough seas and icing *Weather. Extreme cold. Strong wind from north. Visibility 2 nm.* Scout aircraft will illuminate target. Ships with radar 285 may engage outside visibility **Surfaced U Boat detected** bearing green 140 at range 5000 yds from rear ship of close escort | Resolve |
| 6-7 | **AIR ATTACK.** Roll on Air Attack table2. Raid undetected if low level. Other detected at maximum range. *Roll on Soviet/Allied ADTL Cloud* base medium. High attacks will abort. *Weather. Extreme cold. Visibility 1 nm. Choppy seas. Strong wind from SW.* Scout aircraft will illuminate targets. Ships with radar 285 may engage outside visibility **Submerged U Boat** bearing red 170 from rear ship of the centre column at range 2000yds | Proceed |
| 8 | **RE-INFORCEMENTS.** Two British Halcyon class minesweepers of the Kola local escort group join the close escort | Proceed |
| 9 | **AIR ATTACK.** Roll Air Attack table 3. *Cloud base medium Air attacks at high will attack from medium.* Raid detected at maximum radar range. No surprise for low level. *Roll on Soviet/Allied ASTL for fighter cover.* **Weather.** *Extreme cold, visibility 1 nm, choppy seas. Slight wind from SE.* Scout aircraft will illuminate targets. Reduce AA factors by half due to heavy icing. Ships with radar 285 may engage outside visibility **Undetected Submerged U Boat** bearing red 145 from rear ship column one range 1500yds Sonar condition poor reduce detection by 2. Soviet MRB patrol aircraft 3nm behind convoy. | Resolve |
| 0 | **RADAR CONTACT unknown ship** bearing green 90, range 9 miles. Fighting escort already deployed in battle formation on contact side of the convoy if admiralty warning previously received. Detach to intercept. *Weather. Visibility 3 nm. Sea state heavy seas. Snow squalls. High winds from North. Speed of Destroyers and smaller ships reduced to 20 knots maximum.* All destroyer gunnery and torpedo factors reduced by half due to icing and conditions. Cruisers and larger not effected. Roll on *ISB-1.* **Also roll on HF5** | Resolve |

| ★ | SDE 1 SOVIET ARCTIC SUMMER DAYLIGHT EVENTS BOX 1 | Action taken |
|---|---|---|
| 1-5 | **No enemy contact** convoy proceeds | Proceed |
| 6 | **Mines.** One merchant ship strikes a mine. Soviet MBR aircraft will be stationed four miles ahead of the convoy next move. No mutual radio channel available for contact. **WEATHER** Mild. Visibility 10 nm mild sea. Light SE breeze | Resolve |
| 7 | **German Ju290 aircraft** circles the convoy transmitting report. Plus 2 on d10 roll for next move Soviet MBR aircraft will be stationed five miles ahead of the convoy next move. No mutual radio channel available for contact | Combat |
| 8 | **Extra ships.** Minesweeper and small merchant ship (Fish oil carrier) from Karmakuly join convoy | |
| 9 | **AIR ATTACK.** Roll on air attack table 1. **Undetected submerged U Boat** bearing green 90, range 6000yds from rear ship of the convoy **WEATHER** Mild day. Visibility 12nm smooth seas no wind | Combat |
| 0 | **Unknown surface contact** bearing GREEN 10 at 10 miles from lead ship of the escort. Investigate using ISB-Sov. **WEATHER** Extreme cold dull day. Low cloud with some fog banks. Visibility 10 nm mild seas | ISB-Sov |

| ★ | SDE 2 SOVIET ARCTIC SUMMER DAYLIGHT EVENTS BOX 2 | Action taken |
|---|---|---|
| 1-5 | **No enemy contact** convoy proceeds | Proceed |
| 6-7 | **Mines.** One merchant ship strikes a mine. **Undetected submerged U Boat** bearing dead ahead of lead ship range 6000yds **WEATHER** Mild. Visibility 10 nm mild sea. Light SE breeze | Resolve |
| 8-9 | **German Ju290 aircraft** circles the convoy transmitting report. Plus 2 on d10 roll for next move Soviet MBR aircraft will be stationed five miles ahead of the convoy next move. No mutual radio channel available for contact | Combat |

| ★ | SDE 3 SOVIET ARCTIC SUMMER DAYLIGHT EVENTS BOX 3 | Action taken |
|---|---|---|
| 1-5 | **No enemy contact** convoy proceeds | Proceed |
| 6 | **German Ju290 aircraft** circles the convoy transmitting report. Plus 2 on d10 roll for next move Soviet MBR aircraft will be stationed five miles ahead of the convoy next move. No mutual radio channel available for contact | Combat |
| 7-8 | **AIR ATTACK.** Roll on air attack table 2. **WEATHER** Mild day. Visibility 12nm smooth seas no wind | Combat |
| 9 | **Submerged U Boat** bearing dead ahead of lead ship range 6000yds **WEATHER** Mild. Visibility 10 nm mild sea. Light SE breeze | Combat |
| 0 | **Surface contact** bearing GREEN 90 at 15 miles from lead ship of the escort. Investigate using ISB-Sov. **WEATHER** Extreme cold very clear day. Visibility 20 nm mild seas | ISB-Sov |

| ★ | SDE 4 SOVIET ARCTIC SUMMER DAYLIGHT EVENTS BOX 4 | Action taken |
|---|---|---|
| 1-5 | **No enemy contact** convoy proceeds | Proceed |
| 6-7 | **Undetected submerged U Boat** bearing dead ahead of lead ship range 6000yds **WEATHER** Heavy rain Visibility 4 nm rough sea. strong NNE wind | Resolve |
| 7-8 | **AIR ATTACK.** Roll on air attack table 2. **WEATHER** Cold day. Visibility 8nm choppy seas, strong wind from NE | Combat |
| 9 | **AIR ATTACK.** Roll on air attack table 2. **Undetected submerged U Boat** bearing green 90, range 6000yds from rear ship of the convoy **WEATHER** Mild day. Visibility 12nm smooth seas no wind | Combat |
| 0 | **Unknown surface contact** bearing GREEN 10 at 10 miles from lead ship of the escort. Investigate using ISB-Sov. **WEATHER** Extreme cold dull day. Low cloud with some fog banks. Visibility 10 nm mild seas | ISB-Sov |

| ★ | SDE 5 SOVIET ARCTIC SUMMER DAYLIGHT EVENTS BOX 5 | Action taken |
|---|---|---|
| 1-7 | **No enemy contact** convoy proceeds | Proceed |
| 8 | **Mines.** One merchant ship strikes a mine. **WEATHER** Mild. Visibility 10 nm mild sea. Light SE breeze | Resolve |
| 9 | **AIR ATTACK.** Roll on air attack table 2. **WEATHER** Cold day. Visibility 8nm choppy seas, strong wind from NE | Combat |
| 0 | **AIR ATTACK.** Roll on air attack table 3 **WEATHER** Cold day. Visibility 8nm choppy seas, strong wind from NE | Combat |

| ★ | SOVIET SUMMER EVENTS BOX     Arctic twilight. STwE1 | |
|---|---|---|
| 1-3 | **No enemy contact.** Proceed | Destination |
| 4 | **MINEFIELD.** Convoy has entered a German minefield. Test all ships. Roll of 1 on a D10 = mine struck | Resolve |
| 5 | **MINE** One escort has struck a mine. **Unknown surface contact** bearing GREEN 10 at 10 miles from lead ship of the escort. Investigate using ISB-Sov. **WEATHER** Extreme cold dull day. Low cloud with some fog banks. Visibility 10 nm mild seas | Resolve + ISB-Sov |
| 6 | **MINES.** One merchant ship strikes a mine | Resolve |
| 7 | **AIR ATTACK.** Roll on Air Attack table 1. **Weather** Extreme cold. Very clear. Light wind from SE. No clouds. Visibility 6 nm. | Combat |
| 8 | **AIR ATTACK.** Roll on Air Attack table 2. **Weather**. Mild day. High cloud. Visibility 4 nm with light wind from SE. Convoy and close escorts in single file passing through a known minefield via swept channel. | Combat |
| 9-0 | **AIR ATTACK** table 1. **Weather**. Extreme cold rain squalls. Strong wind from NE Visibility 2nm | Combat |
| ★ | SOVIET SUMMER EVENTS BOX     Arctic twilight. STwE2 | |
| 1-3 | **ARRIVAL.** Convoy enters Kola inlet without further incident. | Destination |
| 4 | **MINE.** Convoy enters Kola inlet. One merchant ship strikes a mine. | Resolve |
| 5 | **MINE.** Convoy enters Kola inlet. One close escort strikes a mine. | Resolve |
| 6 | **MINES.** Convoy enters Kola inlet. One close escort and one merchant ship strike mines. | Resolve |
| 7 | **ARRIVAL.** Convoy enters Kola inlet. SEG 2 joins convoy. **AIR ATTACK.** Roll on Air Attack table 4 *Roll on Soviet/Allied AST for fighter cover*. **Weather**. Extreme cold. Very clear. Light wind from SE. No clouds. Visibility 6 nm. | Combat |
| 8 | **ARRIVAL.** Convoy enters Kola inlet. Fighting escort detached to Polyarnoe. After fighting escort detached **AIR ATTACK.** Roll on Air Attack table 4. *Roll on Soviet/Allied AST for fighter cover*. **Weather**. Extreme cold. High cloud. Visibility 4 nm. Convoy and close escorts in single file, following Soviet ice breaker through thin pack ice. All merchant ship AA factors reduced by half due to icing. Warships not effected. | Combat |
| 9-0 | Convoy enters Kola inlet. Fighting escort detached to Polyarnoe. SEG 3 joins convoy. Roll on **AIR ATTACK** table 4. *Roll on Soviet/Allied AST for fighter cover.* **Weather**. Extreme cold. Light snow. Visibility 2nm. | Combat |
| ★ | SOVIET SUMMER EVENTS BOX     Arctic twilight. STwE3 | |
| 1-3 | **ARRIVAL.** Convoy enters Kola inlet without further incident. | Destination |
| 4 | **MINE.** Convoy enters Kola inlet. One merchant ship strikes a mine. | Resolve |
| 5 | **MINE.** Convoy enters Kola inlet. One close escort strikes a mine. | Resolve |
| 6 | **MINES.** Convoy enters Kola inlet. One close escort and one merchant ship strike mines. | Resolve |
| 7 | **ARRIVAL.** Convoy enters Kola inlet. SEG 2 joins convoy. **AIR ATTACK.** Roll on Air Attack table 4 *Roll on Soviet/Allied AST for fighter cover*. **Weather**. Extreme cold. Very clear. Light wind from SE. No clouds. Visibility 6 nm. | Combat |
| 8 | **ARRIVAL.** Convoy enters Kola inlet. Fighting escort detached to Polyarnoe. After fighting escort detached **AIR ATTACK.** Roll on Air Attack table 4. *Roll on Soviet/Allied AST for fighter cover*. **Weather**. Extreme cold. High cloud. Visibility 4 nm. Convoy and close escorts in single file, following Soviet ice breaker through thin pack ice. All merchant ship AA factors reduced by half due to icing. Warships not effected. | Combat |
| 9-0 | Convoy enters Kola inlet. Fighting escort detached to Polyarnoe. SEG 3 joins convoy. Roll on **AIR ATTACK** table 4. *Roll on Soviet/Allied AST for fighter cover.* **Weather**. Extreme cold. Light snow. Visibility 2nm. | Combat |

| D10 | SUMMER ISB-1 — INVESTIGATE A SIGHTING BOX | Time taken | Action |
|---|---|---|---|
| 1-4 | **Neutral** Stopped and examined. Return to convoy | 4 hours | continue |
| 5-6 | **Soviet** merchant ship on independent sailing route | 3 hours | continue |
| 6 | **Soviet SEG 2** joins close escort | 2 hours | Add to convoy |
| 7 | **Soviet SEG 3** joins close escort | 2 hours | Add to convoy |
| 8 | **RESCUE.** Rescue a boat load of survivors from sunken allied merchant ship 5 Victory points | 4 hours | Resolve |
| 9 | **Unknown ship** turns away at full speed. Roll on **runner box** if vessel is to be chased | Runner Box | Runner Box |
| 0 | **ENEMY SURFACE CONTACT**. Roll on Summer Enemy Contact Chart | Combat time | Combat |
| | **SUMMER ISB-2 — INVESTIGATE A SIGHTING BOX** | Time taken | Action |
| 1-3 | **Soviet** merchant ship on independent sailing route | 1 hour | Decision |
| 4-8 | **Soviet SEG 1** joins close escort | 2 hours | Add to convoy |
| 9-0 | **ENEMY SURFACE CONTACT**. Roll on Summer Enemy Contact Chart with +2 to D10 | Combat time | Combat |
| ★ | **SUMMER ISB-Sov — INVESTIGATE A SIGHTING BOX** | Time taken | Action |
| 1-3 | **Soviet** fish factory ship on independent sailing route | 1 hour | Resolve |
| 4-6 | **Soviet** fishing trawler group | 1 hour | Resolve |
| 7-8 | **GERMAN Submarine** visually sighted on the surface at range 10,000yds green 25. The U-boat is carrying out emergency repairs and is unable to dive for five moves | 1 hour | Resolve |
| 9 | **ENEMY SURFACE CONTACT**. Roll on Summer Enemy Contact | Combat time | Combat |
| 0 | **ENEMY SURFACE CONTACT**. Roll on Summer Enemy Contact Chart with +2 to D10 | Combat time | Combat |
| | **SUMMER ISB-3 INVESTIGATE A SIGHTING BOX (Submarine)** | Time taken | Action. |
| 1-3 | **No enemy unit** located | Map move | None |
| 4-8 | **U Boat driven off.** Reduce any Wolfpack attacks during passage by one boat | Map move | None |
| 7 | **U Boat detected** on Asdic/Sonar at range 1,500yds dead ahead at shallow depth | 5 hours | Combat |
| 8 | **GERMAN Submarine surprised** on the surface at range 4,000yds dead ahead while carrying out external repairs. It requires two full moves before it can commence dive | 4 hours | Combat |
| 9 | **Surprise** Submerged submarine will carry out torpedo attack on the searcher from Optimum bearing RED 35 at range 2500yds | 1 Map move | Combat |
| 0 | **GERMAN Submarine** visually sighted on the surface at range 9,000yds red 45. The U-boat is unable to dive for five moves due to Chlorine gas from battery leak. | 1 Map move | Combat |
| | **SUMMER RUNNER BOX** | Time taken | Victory Pts |
| 1-4 | **Ship is a GERMAN Blockade Runner**, which scuttles when fired on. Survivors must be rescued | One event box | 5 |
| 5-6 | **Ship is a GERMAN Blockade Runner**, which will surrender only when hit by gunfire. A Prize crew must be put aboard. Vessel will proceed independently to the nearest Allied port | 1 event box | 10 |
| | **Ship is a Norwegian ore ship** in forced Nazi service that is off course due to storms and damage to navigation equipment. German guards arrested. Ship joins convoy. 10 victory points | 1 event box | 10 |
| 7-0 | **Ship is SWEDISH neutral with contraband cargo**. Prize crew to be put aboard. Ship sent to nearest Allied port. | Two event boxes | 12 |

| D10 | HM 1.   HOME FLEET SUMMER |
|---|---|
| 1-2 | Home fleet too far away to assist |
| 3 | Home fleet can launch **air strike C** to assist and arriving on tactical combat move twenty (60 minutes) of surface action taking place during a twilight move. If night contact HF is unable to assist at all |
| 4 | Home fleet has   detached **CF A** which will arrive from the south on tactical combat move nine (27 minutes) of any action taking place. The rest of the HF is too far away to assist |
| 5 | Home fleet has detached **CF B** which will arrive from the south on tactical combat move nine (27 minutes) of any action taking place |
| 6-7 | Home fleet has   detached **CF C** which will arrive from the south on tactical combat move five (15 minutes) of any action taking place. Home fleet can launch two air strikes to assist, arriving on tactical combat move five (15 minutes) **air strike A** and twelve (36 minutes) **air strike B** of surface action taking place during a twilight move. If any enemy unit slowed to 20 knots or less HF B will arrive within twenty tactical combat moves of action taking place. (60 minutes) |
| 8-9 | Home fleet has been tracking the enemy force. **HF force B** will arrive 15 moves (45 minutes) after combat commences. |
| 0 | Home fleet has been tracking the enemy force. **HF force A** will arrive 10 moves (30 minutes) after combat commences. |

**HOME FLEET TASK FORCES SUMMER**
CF A = Two CA
CF B = One CA and 2 CL
CF C = Three CL
HFB = One BB, one CA, three CL, eight DD
HFA = One BB, one CV, one CA, three CL, nine DD

**SOVIET SUMMER ADDITIONAL ESCORTS JOINING CONVOY**

SEG 1 Three Soviet minesweepers join convoy escort.
SEG 1 Old Liebknecht class destroyer
SEG 3= 1 x Projekt VII destroyer

| D10 | HOME FLEET AIR STRIKES SUMMER | | | | Result |
|---|---|---|---|---|---|
| | 1942 | 1943 | 1944 | 1945 | |
| 1-4 | 6 Swordfish TB 4 Martlet | 8 Albacore TB 6 Martlet fighters | 6 Barracuda TB. 6 Barracuda with 1 heavy bomb 6 Martlet II fighters | 8 Barracuda TB  6 Corsair fighters | Combat |
| 5-7 | 6 Albacore TB 4  Martlet fighters | 9 Albacore TB 6 Martlet fighters | 7 Barracuda TB. 7 Barracuda with 1 heavy bomb 6 Martlet II fighters | 10 Barracuda TB  6 Corsair fighters 4 Firefly as fighter bombers | Combat |
| 8-0 | 8 Albacore TB 6 Seafire fighters | 12 Albacore TB 8 Martlet fighters | 9 Barracuda TB. 9 Avenger with 1 heavy bomb each 8 Corsair fighters | 12 Barracuda TB  8 Martlet II fighters 8 Firefly as fighter bombers | Combat |

| D10 | SUMMER ENEMY CONTACT CHART | | | | Result |
|---|---|---|---|---|---|
| | 1942 | 1943 | 1944 | 1945 | |
| 1-2 | Auxiliary minelayer | Auxiliary minelayer | Auxiliary minelayer | Auxiliary minelayer | Combat |
| 3-4 | 2 x DD + Aux minelayer | Auxiliary minelayer | 3 x T22 TB mine laying | | Combat |
| 5-6 | 3 x DD Mine laying | 3 x T22 TB mine laying | 2 x DD Mine laying | | Combat |
| 7-8 | 3 DD anti shipping patrol | 4 DD anti shipping patrol | 4 DD anti shipping patrol | 2 x T22 TB mine laying | Combat |
| 9-0 | 1 Pocket battleship + 2 DD | 1 Pocket battleship + 3 DD | 1 Pocket battleship,1 CA + 3 DD | | Combat |

## TO HIT TABLE for ASW WEAPONS

### 1941-42. Depth charge Pattern size

| Target depth | Small | Standard | Full | 1942 only Heavy | Air Attack Bomb | Air Attack D/C | Ahead thrown Hedgehog |
|---|---|---|---|---|---|---|---|
| PERISCOPE | 3 | 5 | 6 | - | 2 | 3 | 2 |
| SHALLOW | 3 | 4 | 5 | - | - | 2 | 2 |
| MEDIUM | 2 | 4 | 5 | 6 | - | - | - |
| DEEP | - | 2 | 3 | 4 | - | - | - |
| VERY DEEP | - | - | - | - | - | - | - |
| EXTREME | - | - | - | - | - | - | - |

### 1943 January to June Depth charge Pattern size

| Target depth | Small | Standard | Full | Heavy | Plaster | Creeping | Mk X | Air Attack Bomb | Air Attack D/C | Hedgehog |
|---|---|---|---|---|---|---|---|---|---|---|
| PERISCOPE | 2 | 3 | 6 | - | - | - | - | 2 | 3 | 3 |
| SHALLOW | 2 | 3 | 5 | 7 | - | - | - | - | 2 | 3 |
| MEDIUM | 1 | 2 | 5 | 6 | - | - | - | - | - | 2 |
| DEEP | - | - | 3 | 4 | 6 | 8 | - | - | - | - |
| VERY DEEP | - | - | - | 2 | 4 | 6 | 5 | - | - | - |
| EXTREME | - | - | - | - | - | - | 5 | - | - | - |

### 1943 July to December Depth charge Pattern size

| Target depth | Small | Standard | Full | Plaster | Creeping | Mk X | Air Attack D/C | HH | Single SQUID |
|---|---|---|---|---|---|---|---|---|---|
| PERISCOPE | 3 | 4 | 6 | - | | | 3 | 2 | 2 |
| SHALLOW | 3 | 3 | 5 | - | | | 2 | 2 | 2 |
| MEDIUM | 2 | 2 | 5 | - | | | - | 1 | 2 |
| DEEP | - | 1 | 3 | 6 | 8 | | - | | 1 |
| VERY DEEP | - | - | - | 4 | 6 | 6 | - | | 1 |
| EXTREME | - | - | - | - | - | 6 | | | 1 |

### 1944 January to June Depth charge Pattern size

| Target depth | Small | Standard | Full | Plaster | Creeping | Mk X | Air Attack D/C | Fido | Retro | HH | Twin SQUID | Single SQUID |
|---|---|---|---|---|---|---|---|---|---|---|---|---|
| PERISCOPE | 3 | 5 | 7 | - | | | 3 | 3 | 2 | 2 | 5 | 4 |
| SHALLOW | 3 | 5 | 6 | - | | | 2 | 2 | 2 | 2 | 5 | 4 |
| MEDIUM | 2 | 5 | 6 | - | | | - | 1 | - | 1 | 4 | 3 |
| DEEP | - | 3 | 4 | 6 | 9 | | - | - | - | - | 3 | 2 |
| VERY DEEP | - | - | 1 | 4 | 8 | 6 | - | - | - | - | 3 | 2 |
| EXTREME | - | - | - | - | - | 6 | - | - | - | - | 3 | 2 |

### 1944 July to December Depth charge Pattern size

| Target depth | Small | Standard | Full | Plaster | Creeping | Mk X | Air Attack D/C | Fido | Retro | HH | Twin SQUID | Single SQUID |
|---|---|---|---|---|---|---|---|---|---|---|---|---|
| PERISCOPE | 3 | 5 | 7 | - | | | 3 | 4 | 2 | 3 | 6 | 4 |
| SHALLOW | 3 | 5 | 6 | - | | | 2 | 3 | 2 | 3 | 6 | 4 |
| MEDIUM | 2 | 5 | 6 | - | | | - | 1 | - | 1 | 6 | 3 |
| DEEP | - | 3 | 4 | 7 | 9 | | - | - | - | - | 6 | 3 |
| VERY DEEP | - | - | 1 | 5 | 8 | 6 | - | - | - | - | 5 | 3 |
| EXTREME | - | - | - | 1 | - | 6 | - | - | - | - | 5 | 3 |

### 1945 Depth charge Pattern size

| Target depth | Small | Standard | Full | Plaster | Creeping | Mk X | Air Attack D/C | Fido | Retro | HH | Twin SQUID | Single SQUID |
|---|---|---|---|---|---|---|---|---|---|---|---|---|
| PERISCOPE | 3 | 5 | 7 | - | | | 3 | 5 | 3 | 3 | 9 | 5 |
| SHALLOW | 3 | 5 | 6 | - | | | 2 | 4 | 3 | 3 | 9 | 5 |
| MEDIUM | 2 | 5 | 6 | - | | | - | 1 | - | 1 | 9 | 5 |
| DEEP | - | 3 | 4 | 7 | 9 | | - | - | - | - | 9 | 5 |
| VERY DEEP | - | - | 1 | 5 | 8 | 6 | - | - | - | - | 8 | 4 |

## DAMAGE CAUSED TO SUBMARINES Roll D10, and consult table by looking down the appropriate column

| D10 | SURFACE SHIP WEAPONS | | | | | AIRCRAFT ASW WEAPONS | | | | | SURFACE GUNNERY | | |
|---|---|---|---|---|---|---|---|---|---|---|---|---|---|
| | Depth charge | Mk X | Hedge Hog Mouse trap | Squid | Towed ASW | Fido | Retro bomb | ASW Bomb | Air rocket | Strafe | 4"Shark 4.5"-6" | 12pdr 3"-4.1" | AA |
| 1 | AW | BU | CPQX | JVOR | O | WRPD | VU | E | FV | E | FV | V | E |
| 2 | BV | AV | WXUJ | BODV | L | Y | QPV | F | GW | N | DEH | DE | N |
| 3 | CD | CX | Y | APWQ | B | Y | GHJO | FV | EFL | MO | GHS | OND | MO |
| 4 | HV | WHP | Y | Y | R | Y | DEGIV | IV | NMGW | LE | GEV | RSO | LE |
| 5 | WX | AHO | Y | Y | P | Z | QPRW | PV | GMOX | LO | GEW | FLE | LO |
| 6 | UQ | WUDO | Y | Z | E | Z | Y | QV | NPRS | UE | SMEW | FIL | UE |
| 7 | JV | PQWI | T | Z | D | Z | Y | OV | DKUV | R | KGEL | GME | R |
| 8 | OP | Y | Z | Z | OD | Z | Y | EOV | T | MN | KPGL | GHR | MN |
| 9 | Y | Y | Z | Z | EL | T | Z | PUV | T | NE | T | MLS | NE |
| 0 | Z | Z | Z | T | C | T | Z | WJ | Z | SM | T | USM | SM |

### SUBMARINE DAMAGE TYPES

| | | | |
|---|---|---|---|
| A | Forced to dive 2 levels out of control. Check for crush | N | Gun crews killed. One move to replace them |
| B | Forced to dive 1 level out of control | O | One periscope KO |
| C | Out of control. Rise 2 levels. If it breaks surface it will take 2 moves to dive again | P | Engineering damage. Two knots speed loss from submerged speed |
| D | Fuel leak on surface | Q | Hydrophones knocked out |
| E | One AA point knocked out | R | Rudder damaged. Circling out of control until repaired |
| F | Engineering damage. 2 knots from surface speed | S | Ready use ammunition explosion. Serious fire. All guns and gun crews KO |
| G | Engineering damage. 5 knots from surface speed | T | Internal explosion. Submarine sinking |
| H | Two torpedo tubes KO. Serious Flooding | U | Dive planes damaged. Double time to rise or dive |
| I | One torpedo tube KO. Minor Flooding | V | Minor Flooding |
| J | Critical equipment damage. Return to base | W | Major flooding. Pumps running. Add one to detection due to noise until repaired |
| K | Pressure hull damaged. Can't dive. Critical flooding | X | Cannot operate below medium depth |
| L | Deck gun knocked out | Y | Forced to surface in sinking condition |
| M | Command crew killed. Circles out of control | Z | Destroyed |

| | |
|---|---|
| Cross off 1 for minor flooding | 4 for Major flooding |
| 2 for serious flooding | 8 for Critical flooding |

## Torpedo to hit table.

Work out the angle of the target at the time torpedo is fired. If it is fired within 2000yds it will reach the target in the same move. The number shown is therefore the percentage chance to hit.

If the torpedo arrives on the second move, consider the angle from the point where it was fired and the angle shows which chart. The number shown is therefore the percentage chance to hit, but the size of target is reduced down one.

If the torpedo arrives on the third move, again work out the angle and consult the appropriate chart. The size of target is reduced one further level down.

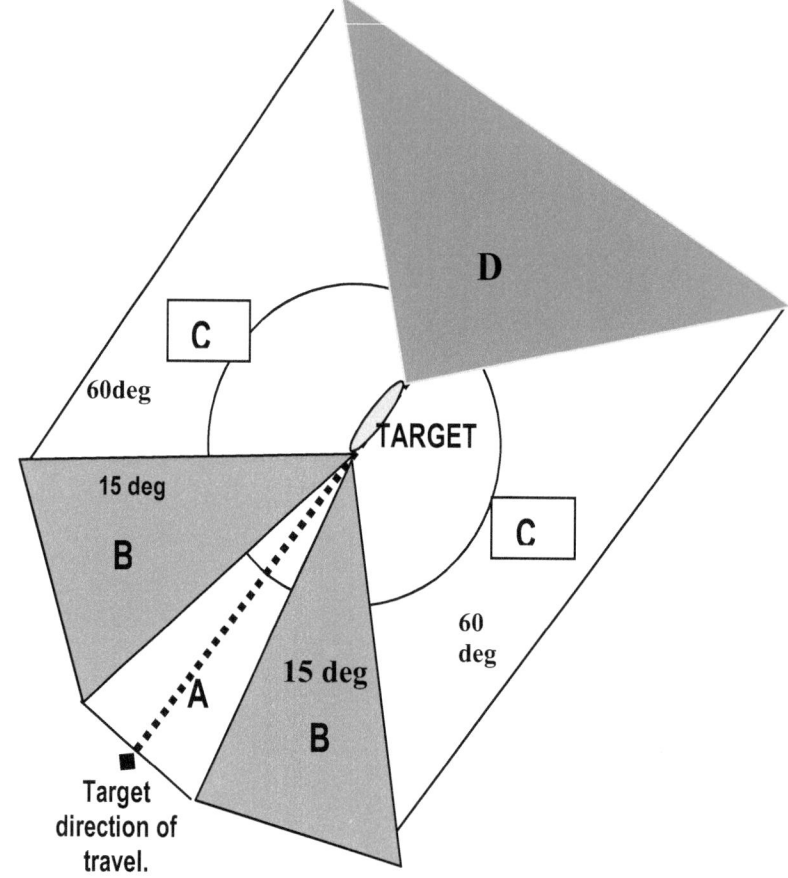

| | TABLE A | Target speed in knots | | | | | | | |
|---|---|---|---|---|---|---|---|---|---|
| Target | 0 | 2-5 | 6-10 | 11-15 | 16-20 | 21-25 | 26-30 | 31-35 | 36-40 |
| Very Large | 5 | 4 | 3 | 3 | 2 | 2 | 1 | 1 | 1 |
| Large | 4 | 3 | 3 | 2 | 2 | 1 | 1 | 1 | 1 |
| Medium | 4 | 3 | 2 | 2 | 2 | 2 | 2 | - | - |
| Small | 3 | 2 | 2 | 1 | 1 | - | - | - | - |
| Very small | 3 | 2 | 1 | - | - | - | - | - | - |

| | TABLE B | Target speed in knots | | | | | | | |
|---|---|---|---|---|---|---|---|---|---|
| Target | 0 | 2-5 | 6-10 | 11-15 | 16-20 | 21-25 | 26-30 | 31-35 | 36-40 |
| Very Large | 8 | 7 | 6 | 5 | 4 | 4 | 3 | 2 | 2 |
| Large | 6 | 6 | 5 | 5 | 4 | 3 | 3 | 2 | 1 |
| Medium | 6 | 5 | 5 | 4 | 3 | 2 | 2 | 1 | - |
| Small | 5 | 4 | 4 | 3 | 3 | 2 | - | - | - |
| Very small | 4 | 3 | 3 | 2 | 2 | 1 | - | - | - |

| | TABLE C | Target speed in knots | | | | | | | |
|---|---|---|---|---|---|---|---|---|---|
| Target size | 0 | 2-5 | 6-10 | 11-15 | 16-20 | 21-25 | 26-30 | 31-35 | 36-40 |
| Very Large | 6 | 5 | 5 | 4 | 3 | 3 | 2 | 1 | - |
| Large | 5 | 4 | 4 | 3 | 3 | 2 | 2 | 1 | - |
| Medium | 4 | 4 | 3 | 3 | 2 | 1 | - | - | - |
| Small | 3 | 3 | 2 | 2 | 1 | 1 | - | - | - |
| Very small | 2 | 2 | 1 | 1 | - | - | - | - | - |

| | TABLE D | Target speed in knots | | | | | | | |
|---|---|---|---|---|---|---|---|---|---|
| Target size | 0 | 2-5 | 6-10 | 11-15 | 16-20 | 21-25 | 26-30 | 31-35 | 36-40 |
| Very Large | 5 | 4 | 3 | 2 | 1 | - | - | - | - |
| Large | 4 | 3 | 3 | 2 | 1 | - | - | - | - |
| Medium | 3 | 2 | 1 | 1 | 1 | - | - | - | - |
| Small | 2 | 2 | 1 | 1 | - | - | - | - | - |
| Very small | 1 | 1 | 1 | - | - | - | - | -1 | - |

**Range**

These tables assume targets are within 4,000 yds of the firing point. If targets are beyond that distance, move one column to the right for chance to hit, PER ADDITIONAL 4000yds.
*(Example move two columns left for a target between 8 and 12 thousand yards)*

**Japanese 24" torpedoes**

These tables assume a target is within 8,000yds of the firing point. They are moved one column to the right for each additional 8,800yds.

| Torpedo damage table. For mines +1 to die roll. | | | | | | | | | | |
|---|---|---|---|---|---|---|---|---|---|---|
| type | Die score | | | | | | | | | |
|  | 1 | 2 | 3 | 4 | 5 | 6 | 7 | 8 | 9 | 0 |
| BBA | IV | IV | EJ | CEJ | EKX | AEK | LWG | BLW | GW | F |
| BBM | I | JW | KW | KX | KWX | AEL | AHL | LWX | ZB | F |
| BB BC | JW | JW | JWX | LAV | LWX | LEV | APW | Z | Y | F |
| CA | WI | KW | KXA | LAV | LNW | IWX | AOW | XY | XZ | F |
| CL | WI | KW | KXA | LAW | LNW | JWX | APW | F | 4 | 6 |
| CV | JV | JV | JVX | JVU | JWT | KWT | LWT | LHW | Z | F |
| CVE | WI | KW | KXU | KVU | KNW | LWT | MWX | MEV | Z | F |
| DD | LW | MW | MNZ | Y | ZX | 4 | 5 | 6 | 6 | 6 |
| PG | MW | YW | ZW | Z4 | 4 | 5 | 6 | 6 | 6 | 6 |
| PGE | 4 | 5 | 5 | 5 | 5 | 6 | 6 | 6 | 6 | 6 |
| TR SS | 5 | 6 | 6 | 6 | 6 | 6 | 6 | 6 | 6 | 6 |
| AUX | LWX | LWX | LWX | YW | ZX | Z2 | 4 | 5 | 6 | 7.6 |
| AO | KX | KX | LX | MX | YX1 | ZX2 | 4X | 5X | 8 | 67 |
| AE | KX | LX | MX | 4 | 5 | 6 | 8 | 7 | 7 | 7 |
| AP | JV3 | KV3 | KV1 | KV2 | LWX | Y | Z | 4 | 5 | 6 |
| AC | KV3 | MW | Y | Z | 5 | 8 | 6 | 6 | 6 | 6 |
| AB | KV3 | MW | 5 | 5 | 6 | 6 | 6 | 6 | 6 | 6 |
| AK | KV3 | KV1 | KV2 | Z | Y | 4 | 5 | 5 | 6 | 6 |

**DAMAGE FROM TORPEDOES**
Cross reference type with D10 roll.
The cross reference column may show one or more letters or a number. If there is more than one letter, it represents the total damage suffered from the hit. For example KXA would mean the ship suffered the three damages K, X and A.
**NOTE**
AIR DROPPED and all 18"torpedoes are moved one column to the LEFT when checking damages

## DAMAGE SUFFERED FROM TORPEDO AND BOMB HITS

| | | | |
|---|---|---|---|
| A | One gun mount KO. Roll for which. | R | Critical fire amidships. 2 AA points destroyed. |
| B | Two gun mounts KO. Roll for forward or aft. | S | Major flooding. Fuel oil leaking. |
| C | Secondary gun mount KO | T | Hangar. If carrier there may be more than one hangar. Roll for percentage of aircraft lost. Critical fire. |
| D | 2 AA points destroyed. | U | Catapult. One aircraft catapult K.O. If aircraft aboard, one is destroyed. Serious fire. |
| E | Serious flooding | V | Serious flooding. Minor fire. |
| F | Magazine hit. Roll D10. 1-3 = Fwd magazine flooded. 4-6 = Aft magazine flooded. 7-9 central or secondary magazines flooded. 0 = Magazine detonation. Ship blows up. If magazines flooded appropriate guns are out of action & critical flooding. If a magazine is already flooded it cannot suffer a detonation hit | W | Serious flooding. Fuel oil leak. |
| G | Vitals. Roll D10. 1.2.3.4. = power lost to fwd guns. .5.6.7.8 = aft guns until repaired. + Critical flooding 10 knots speed loss | X | Major Fire on upper deck amidships. 5 AA points destroyed. |
| H | Steering. Critical flooding. Steering damaged. Out of control port 1.2.3.4. Starboard 5.6.7.8. Ahead 9.0 | Y | Critical flooding forward. Engineering damage. Can't steam. Can be towed by the stern only. |
| I | Engineering 1 knot speed loss | Z | Critical flooding aft. Ship comes to a stop. Can be towed. |
| J | Engineering 3 knots speed loss | 1 | Forward cargo holds damaged. |
| K | Engineering 5 knots speed loss | 2 | Aft cargo holds damage. |
| L | Engineering ship can no longer make more than half its original speed | 3 | Cargo. Central hold damaged. |
| M | Engineering ship comes to a stop until repaired | 4 | Fatal hull damage. Ship is crippled and sinking very slowly. Cannot be saved. It can be finished off by other ships. |
| N | Engineering all Radar, sonar, searchlights, lose power until repaired | 5 | Fatal hull damage. Abandon ship. Vessel is sinking steadily. |
| O | Electronics. Roll D6. 1.2= gunnery radar. 3.4=surface radar. 5.6 = air warning radar Unable to be repaired | 6 | Fatal hull damage, ship sinks rapidly. |
| P | Electronics. Wireless/signal bridge hit. K.O. Second hit = TBS KO. 3rd Hit = visual signals KO | 7 | Ammunition ship or tanker with petrol. Cargo explodes. Ship vaporised. |
| Q | ASW hit. D/Charge system KO. Roll D 10. Score of 1 -3 = detonation, fatal damage and ship sinking by stern | 8 | Ship burning fiercely, but sinking very slowly. Illuminates area around it and providing background light silhouette for other ships. |

**GNAT.** The T5 Zaunkonig was a homing torpedo that was set to be attracted to the pitch and sound of escort vessels. It would not home on merchant ships due to their lower tone of engine, propeller noise and speed. After initial combat tests it was mistakenly believed by the Germans, that there were a very high percentage of hits. This was not actually the case. The U Boats usually fired the weapon in situations of danger and stress, and then dived without actually seeing the results. Because of this detonations were often though to have been hits, but in reality the torpedoes had malfunction or detonated in the wake of the target. The weapon was known to the Allies as GNAT. U Boats initially carried two of these weapons from September 1943, but this was increased to four in late 1944, with three forward and one aft. Gnat was intended for use against escorts at the speed they would normally be moving at while part of a screen. Because of the slow speed of Gnat it was unable to catch ships moving at more than 18 knots and it was set such that it would not be attracted by ships travelling at less than 10 knots.

## To hit and Damage chart for GNAT Anti Escort torpedo hits

GNAT can only be fired at a target within 6000yds. It does not become effective until it has travelled 400yds from the firer.
Targets of speed 19 knots or more are immune. Ships at 9 knots or less are also immune

| D10 | Damage caused |
|---|---|
| 1-4 | Torpedo missed or malfunctioned |
| 5-6 | Torpedo detonated in wake. No damage |
| 8 | **Major flooding** Torpedo detonated prematurely. Engineering damage 5 knots speed loss All aft ASW equipment out of action |
| 9 | **Critical flooding.** Stern blown off. Cannot steam. Can be towed or scuttled. All weapons and electronics knocked out. **Major fire** |
| 0 | **Fatal hull damage.** Abandon ship. Vessel will sink in D12 moves. |

**ANTI GNAT DEVICE.** Because of early successes the Allies quickly developed a counter to GNAT. This was known as the **FOXER** and was a towed noise maker. After sea trials the RN double Foxer was found unnecessary and the Canadian single version was adopted instead. If players wish to deploy Foxer in games from mid 1943 onward they must declare it by ticking foxer section of the ship damage form. If attacked by an acoustic torpedo such as Gnat the ship rolls for hits against it by reducing the D10 roll by two. Similarly it reduces its own ASW search value by roll by 1

## Pattern running torpedoes FAT and FAT2

**FAT** or Federapparat was a pattern running torpedo that ran a zigzag course after being fired. The intent was to allow a U Boat to fire it into a convoy without needing to penetrate the screen or aim for a specific ship. Once fired the weapon proceeded for a set distance, then performed a sharp turn and with subsequent turns moved back and forth through the columns of ships at a speed of around 7.5 knots. It was considered that FAT could reduce the risk of the attacking boat being detected as by 1943 it was becoming difficult for U Boats to approach close enough for optimum shots. It used a basic G7a T1 torpedo with Federapparat system fitted. In use FAT was fired at the flanks of a convoy and was unable to be used against a head on target. It achieved its first sinking in December of 1942.

**FAT 2.** This employed the Federapparat system on the T3a electric torpedo. Performance was similar to the original FAT but it could be fired from dead ahead to zigzag across the course of oncoming ships, especially escorts in a screen across the front of a convoy. This torpedo can be used from September 1943 onward

In practice FAT did score some hits but were not as accurate as an aimed torpedo.

LUT was a late war version in very limited use during 1945. It was a much longer range torpedo.

### USING FAT

Nominate one ship within 4000yds as the target point. The move after the torpedo was fired test if against the target ship with a roll of 1 on a d10 to hit. If no hit it is tested again on the second move after firing. This time it is tested against a target within 1000yds to port or starboard of the original target ship, and between 500- 750yds to its rear. The firer nominates at the time of firing, which way the torpedo will move. Again the hit chance is a roll of 1 on a D10. If it does not hit it is tested again against a target within 1000yds port or starboard of the second target and again at least 500-750yds to its rear. Once again the chance to hit is a 1 on a D10. If the FAT has not hit by then it is considered to have sunk.

**SIGHTING when using the original FAT** in daylight conditions. If it misses the first target roll a d10. On a score of 5-0 the torpedo has been sighted. Other ships will take evasive action and there will be no further hit rolls. The same is repeated for the second target.

**SIGHTING When using FAT2.** This was a wake less electric torpedo and cannot be sighted.

## RAMMING AND COLLISION TABLES

To the left of the slash is damage to the submarine or ship rammed. To the right of the slash is damage sustained by the ramming ship. Ships that collide and ships that ram submarines use the torpedo damage chart.

| | RAMMING SUBMARINES | | | |
|---|---|---|---|---|
| | Glancing blow | Rammed squarely. | Rammed bow or stern angle | Rammed while diving |
| 1 | AO / D | KGD / SN | AV/ D | HD / DI |
| 2 | AQ / D | KGH / EN | DIQ/ D | CDV / DI |
| 3 | AI / D | KGR / EN | RV/ D | EFV / EJ |
| 4 | BD / D | KGN / EN | GV/ D | GIJ / EJ |
| 5 | BP / DI | KLM / HN | WX/ DJ | JOV / DH |
| 6 | BPF / DJ | T / LVN | OPQ/ KS | LOU / EH |
| 7 | W / JV | Z / LVN | JID/ KS | OR W/ EK |
| 8 | WU/ S | Z / LSN | FJW/ KS | DWX / SJ |
| 9 | XLJ/ S | Z / WMN | K/ LS | Y / SNJ |
| 0 | Z / WN | Z / YN | Z / Y | Z / LN |

Damage to submarine (Damage to submarines chart) / Damage to ramming ship. Torpedo damage chart.

| | Collision between surface ships | | | |
|---|---|---|---|---|
| | Glancing blow | Rammed squarely. | Rammed bow angle | Rammed stern angle |
| 1 | D / D | WK / VI | S/S | KS / SI |
| 2 | D / D | WH / VI | KS / KS | KV / SJ |
| 3 | DI / DI | WK / VJ | KS / KS | LH / VJ |
| 4 | E/E | WL / VJ | WM / WM | LH / WK |
| 5 | E/E | WL / WJ | WM / WM | LH / WK |
| 6 | E/E | WMN / WJ | WM / WM | M / WJ |
| 7 | V / V | Y / WK | WMN / WMN | M / WK |
| 8 | V / V | Z / WK | Y / Y | Z / WK |
| 9 | W / W | Z / Y | Y / Y | ZQ / Y |
| 0 | W / W | Z / Y | Y / Y | Z Q/ Y |

Damage to ship rammed (Torpedo damage chart) / Damage to ramming ship. (Torpedo damage chart)

NOTE. Damaged ships can be scuttled with depth charges. A small pattern is expended. Damage is rolled for as if it was a torpedo.

Refer the letters to the damage chart.
Note that ships may be shown with more than one letter to reflect the extent of damage.

## SHIP AA FIRE

Each ship is shown with an AA fire power for long, medium and close range. The number shown is the percentage chance to hit a single aircraft at long or medium range. If a hit is scored, consult the HIT RESULTS chart for damage caused.

**Close range factors** can be divided into two or more to allow engaging more than one aircraft if wished. Therefore a ship with an AA value of 20 could fire on three aircraft splitting the chances to the nearest divisor of 20, to use 07 on each. However NOTE below re firing to both sides. A few ships may show 100 or more as their fire factor. This may be an automatic hit, but of course the damage may not result in an automatic kill. Such numbers make it easier for these ships to split their fire factor to engage more aircraft.

**LONG RANGE and MEDIUM range** factors can be divided up into two, only if the ship firing has more than one director.

**MEDIUM LEVEL ATTACKS** Only half the close range factor can be used against aircraft making straight and level attacks at medium level.

**HIGH LEVEL ATTACKS** This form of bombing attack was rarely used against convoys by the Luftwaffe because the chances to hit a moving ship were very poor. Instead they preferred low level, medium level, or dive bombing. However if a player should opt to bomb from this level the attackers can only be engaged by AA fire at medium and close ranges. The AA factor of any ship at this range is determined as 02.5 for each single heavy AA and 05 for each twin heavy AA mount. Therefore a ship with four twin AA mounts able to bear, would have a hi level AA fire of 20%. A ship with a single heavy AA would have a hi level AA fire of 2%. A ship with two single heavy AA mounts would have 5% (02.5 + 02.5) Two twin heavy AA mounts able to bear would total 10%.

**Attacks from two directions**

Close range AA factors have been sided and centre lined when considering the strength. However as they are sided, there is always a spare ½ the value, to fire to the opposite side if a ship is being attacked from more than one direction.

For example a ship with a close range AA value of 20 could use that and also fire half as much (10) to the opposite side without penalty.

**FIRING DIRECTLY AHEAD OR ASTERN** Ships engaging aircraft attacking from the bow or stern arc use only half their AA factor at the applicable ranges. However in some special instances a ship damage chart may show that a vessel has no ahead or astern fire if that is applicable. This is often the case with submarines that only have their AA mounts on the rear of their conning tower.

**MERCHANT-SHIPS.** Most merchant ships have been given a standard AA firepower for game simplicity. However you will see on some damage charts that there are exceptions to this. CAM ships usually have more AA power and a few others too, which keeps the attacking player uncertain as to what he will face.

## AA and air to air firing damage

**DEST** = Destroyed. Aircraft blew up in mid air.

**DAM** = Damaged. Aircraft will continue with its attack. Reduce bombing accuracy by 1 and the ATA by half. If damaged twice it will crash

**DROFF** = Aircraft has been driven off. Will not attack or continue to shadow. It will break off and return to base. Fighters will also break off action. Can only engage in ATA if it is attacked

**CRL** = Aircraft crash lands on the water near an escort determined by a random die roll. The escort must perform a rescue of the crew. Even the enemy are useful, especially for interrogation back at base.

**TA** = Turn away. Aircraft suffered minor damage OR the accuracy of the AA fire forced the pilot to break off the attack. The aircraft can then come in a second time. If the same aircraft suffers two TA results in a row it must abort the attack and return to base. If it suffers three TA results non-consecutively it must abort the attack and return to base.

## AIR TO AIR COMBAT

Refer to chart. Cross reference the aircraft in combat. The number shown is the score required on a D10 for the **ALLIED** aircraft to get first shot. A higher score results in the **AXIS** aircraft winning first shot.

Pursuit and subsequent combat may take place, but no SINGLE engine aircraft may engage more than three times during any one mission. Twin and MULTI ENGINE aircraft may engage four times during any one mission.

Once it is determined which aircraft gets the first shot, it is referred to the **HIT RESULTS CHART**

The air combat chart includes aircraft not mentioned in the game so that players may substitute aircraft models if they do not have those specified in the events boxes.

### HIT RESULT CHART

| D10 score | Close range AA fire. | LR & MR AA fire. | ATA |
|---|---|---|---|
| 1 | DROFF | TA | DROFF |
| 2 | DROFF | TA | DROFF |
| 3 | DROFF | DROFF | DROFF |
| 4 | DAM | DROFF | DROFF |
| 5 | DAM | DAM | DAM |
| 6 | DAM | DAM | DAM |
| 7 | CRL | DAM | DAM |
| 8 | DEST | DEST | DEST |
| 9 | DEST | DEST | DEST |
| 0 | DEST | DEST | DEST |

## AIR ATTACK METHOD

Aircraft models are placed at the edge of the playing area on the bearing indicated which is taken from the nearest edge of the convoy columns. Most air contacts start at a range stated in the event boxes.
(1) If AA fire or air interception is to take place at long range, that is then resolved.
(2) AA fire or air interception at medium range is then resolved.
(3) Aircraft are moved to their target. Close range AA fire is then resolved. If aircraft are at Medium level this is halved
(4) Bombing takes place and results determined
(5) Aircraft then move according to their speed. This may be to the next target. If able to move further note attacks that took place and place air model at the distance it reached
(6) If any bombing took place this is now resolved
(7) AA fire at aircraft takes place according to the range they are now at
(8) Sequences continue until aircraft are out of range/visibility and attacks and interceptions are completed

**BOMBING** These tables show the chance to roll for damage, per attack. The number of actual hits that may have been achieved is reflected in the damage ultimately inflicted, as well as the success of the hit/hits. Aircraft are shown with a number of 'attacks' not individual bombs

### DIVE BOMBING — Target speed in knots

| Target size | 0-5 | 6-10 | 11-20 | 21-30 | 31-40 |
|---|---|---|---|---|---|
| Very Large | 7 | 7 | 6 | 3 | - |
| Large | 7 | 6 | 5 | 2 | - |
| Medium | 4 | 4 | 3 | 1 | - |
| Small | 3 | 3 | 2 | 1 | - |
| Very small | 4 | 2 | 2 | 1 | - |

### LOW LEVEL BOMBING — Target speed in knots

| Target size | 0-5 | 6-10 | 11-20 | 21-30 | 31-40 |
|---|---|---|---|---|---|
| Very Large | 6 | 6 | 5 | 4 | 2 |
| Large | 5 | 5 | 4 | 3 | 2 |
| Medium | 3 | 3 | 3 | 2 | 1 |
| Small | 2 | 2 | 2 | 1 | 1 |
| Very small | 2 | 1 | 1 | 1 | 1 |

### MEDIUM LEVEL BOMBING — Target speed in knots

| Target size | 0-5 | 6-10 | 11-20 | 21-30 | 31-40 |
|---|---|---|---|---|---|
| Very Large | 4 | 3 | 2 | 1 | 1 |
| Large | 3 | 2 | 2 | 1 | 1 |
| Medium | 2 | 2 | 1 | 1 | - |
| Small | 1 | 1 | 1 | - | - |
| Very small | 1 | - | - | - | - |

### HIGH LEVEL BOMBING — Target speed in knots

| Target size | 0-5 | 6-10 | 11-20 | 21-30 | 31-40 |
|---|---|---|---|---|---|
| Very Large | 1 | 1 | 1 | - | - |
| Large | 1 | 1 | 1 | - | - |
| Medium | 1 | 1 | -- | - | - |
| Small | 1 | 1 | - | - | - |
| Very small | 1 | - | - | - | - |

### BOMB ATTACKS
Air attacks are rated as Light. Medium or Heavy Use the hit damage chart to find the type of damage scored Use the BOMBING AND GUNNERY DAMAGE chart to establish those damages

### SHIP RADAR
On the ship damage charts, radar detection for aircraft has been abbreviated
SA = Single aircraft   SLFA = Single low flying aircraft
AF = Air formation.

### Hit Damage Tables

| Ship type | 1 | 2 | 3 | 4 | 5 | 6 | 7 | 8 | 9 | 0 |
|---|---|---|---|---|---|---|---|---|---|---|
| **HIT DAMAGE FROM LIGHT BOMB ATTACKS** | | | | | | | | | | |
| BBA BBM | - | - | - | S | C | N | M | B | G | S |
| BB BC | - | S | R | C | C | N | M | B | G | S |
| CA/ CL | C | C | R | M | N | F | B | G | S | T |
| CV /CVE | C | C | G | G | GH | H | H | H | H | HC |
| DD PG | - | G | G | H | AH | AI | ACI | F | P | U |
| PGE PCE AM | - | G | F | H | H | HS | IS | IS | JV |
| TR AUX SS | G | H | H | H | V | IV | HV | FV | W | W |
| AO AE AC | G | H | C | S | SH | SH | TH | TI | J | US |
| AP AB AK | G | H | H | H | I | I | J | J | J | T |
| **HIT DAMAGE FROM MEDIUM BOMB ATTACKS** | | | | | | | | | | |
| BBA BBM | G | G | G | C | C | C | B | B | F | M |
| BB BC | G | G | C | F | C | H | B | H | H | I |
| CA/ CL | G | B | C | B | CB | AF | HS | PN | R | TH |
| CV / CVE | G | C | C | S | CS | HS | HT | IT | Q | FR |
| DD PG | G | H | I | I | JP | VA | OA | PW | F | D |
| PGE PCE AM | G | H | H | H | JU | JV | KV | KW | X | Z |
| TR AUX SS | H | IU | IU | IV | JW | KW | YCA | XCA | Z | Z |
| AO AE AC | G | I | C | TI | TH | THU | TIU | TJV | X | Z |
| AP AB AK | G | IW | IS | IV | JS | ITU | JTU | JTV | Y | Z |
| **HIT DAMAGE FROM HEAVY BOMB ATTACKS** | | | | | | | | | | |
| BBA BBM | G | H | CB | CS | BHS | AHT | EI | WI | WJ | FJ |
| BB BC | H | I | IC | CB | CAB | AIT | EJ | WJ | EL | DK |
| CA/ CL | H | IS | JSP | BH | FJB | FTA | JSA | KSP | XS | YTD |
| CV /CVE | H | T | TR | BI | FJW | CE | JQS | QRT | XT | YTD |
| DD PG | I | WI | 0T | EP | ACE | AM | DP | Z | Z | Z |
| PGE PCE AM | JS | JF | WO | AJ | WTA | YT | D | Z | Z | Z |
| TR AUX SS | W | WI | KT | XS | YTC | Z | Z | Z | Z | Z |
| AO AE AC | W | JS | JT | TK | X | Y | Z | Z | Z | Z |
| AP AB AK | W | W | WH | WI | X | Y | Z | Z | Z | Z |

| AIR COMBAT CHART 1 | Do17 | Do217 | He111 | Ju87 | Ju88A | He 177 | Ju290 | Fw200 | Ar 196 | Bv222 | Ju52 |
|---|---|---|---|---|---|---|---|---|---|---|---|
| Albacore | 5 | 5 | 5 | 4 | 5 | 5 | 5 | 5 | 5 | 3 | 6 |
| Barracuda | 6 | 5 | 6 | 5 | 5 | 5 | 5 | 5 | 5 | 6 | 8 |
| Catalina | 4 | 4 | 5 | 4 | 4 | 4 | 4 | 4 | 5 | 5 | 7 |
| Fulmar | 7 | 6 | 7 | 6 | 6 | 6 | 6 | 7 | 6 | 7 | 9 |
| Firefly | 6 | 6 | 7 | 6 | 6 | 6 | 6 | 6 | 7 | 7 | 9 |
| Hurricane | 8 | 7 | 8 | 7 | 7 | 7 | 7 | 8 | 7 | 8 | 9 |
| Martlet | 7 | 6 | 7 | 7 | 6 | 6 | 6 | 7 | 7 | 7 | 9 |
| Martlet II | 8 | 7 | 8 | 7 | 7 | 7 | 7 | 8 | 9 | 9 | 9 |
| P40 | 8 | 7 | 8 | 7 | 7 | 7 | 7 | 8 | 6 | 7 | 9 |
| P47 | 8 | 7 | 8 | 7 | 7 | 7 | 7 | 8 | 6 | 7 | 9 |
| Seafire | 8 | 7 | 8 | 7 | 7 | 7 | 7 | 8 | 9 | 9 | 9 |
| Sea Hurricane | 8 | 7 | 8 | 7 | 7 | 7 | 7 | 8 | 7 | 7 | 9 |
| Swordfish | 5 | 4 | 5 | 4 | 4 | 4 | 4 | 5 | 4 | 3 | 5 |
| Walrus | 2 | 1 | 2 | 1 | 1 | 2 | 2 | 3 | 3 | 3 | 5 |
| I-152 – I 16 | 6 | 5 | 6 | 6 | 5 | 5 | 5 | 6 | 6 | 8 | 9 |
| Be2 | 3 | 4 | 3 | 3 | 4 | 4 | 4 | 3 | 3 | 4 | 6 |
| IL-2 | 6 | 5 | 6 | 6 | 5 | 5 | 5 | 6 | 6 | 7 | 8 |
| IL-4 | 5 | 4 | 5 | 4 | 4 | 4 | 4 | 5 | 5 | 6 | 7 |
| LaGG-3 | 7 | 6 | 6 | 6 | 6 | 6 | 6 | 7 | 7 | 8 | 9 |
| MiG 3 | 6 | 5 | 6 | 5 | 5 | 5 | 5 | 6 | 6 | 7 | 9 |
| Pe2 / Pe3 | 7 | 6 | 7 | 6 | 6 | 6 | 6 | 7 | 6 | 7 | 8 |
| SB-2 | 4 | 3 | 4 | 3 | 3 | 3 | 3 | 4 | 4 | 5 | 7 |
| Yak 7 | 7 | 6 | 7 | 7 | 6 | 6 | 6 | 7 | 7 | 8 | 9 |
| Yak-9 | 8 | 7 | 8 | 7 | 7 | 7 | 7 | 8 | 8 | 8 | 9 |

| AIR COMBAT CHART 2 | Bf109 | Fw190 | Me110 | Me210 | He219 | Ju88C | Ju188 | Ju86 | He115 | Do18 | Bv138 |
|---|---|---|---|---|---|---|---|---|---|---|---|
| Albacore | 2 | 1 | 3 | 2 | 2 | 3 | 3 | 5 | 4 | 6 | 5 |
| Barracuda | 3 | 3 | 4 | 3 | 3 | 4 | 3 | 6 | 7 | 6 | 6 |
| Catalina | 2 | 1 | 3 | 2 | 2 | 4 | 2 | 5 | 4 | 5 | 5 |
| Fulmar | 4 | 3 | 5 | 3 | 3 | 6 | 3 | 6 | 6 | 8 | 7 |
| Firefly | 4 | 4 | 5 | 4 | 4 | 5 | 4 | 6 | 6 |  |  |
| Hurricane | 5 | 5 | 6 | 5 | 5 | 8 | 5 | 7 | 7 | 8 | 7 |
| Martlet | 5 | 5 | 6 | 5 | 5 | 7 | 5 | 8 | 7 | 8 | 8 |
| Martlet II | 6 | 6 | 7 | 6 | 6 | 7 | 6 | 9 | 8 | 8 | 7 |
| P40 | 5 | 4 | 6 | 5 | 5 | 6 | 5 | 9 | 7 | 8 | 7 |
| P47 | 6 | 6 | 7 | 6 | 6 | 7 | 6 | 9 | 8 | 8 | 7 |
| Seafire. | 5 | 4 | 7 | 6 | 6 | 7 | 6 | 9 | 7 | 8 | 7 |
| Sea Hurricane | 5 | 4 | 6 | 5 | 5 | 7 | 5 | 8 | 7 | 8 | 7 |
| Swordfish | 1 | 1 | 4 | 3 | 3 | 5 | 3 | 6 | 4 | 5 | 4 |
| Walrus | 1 | 1 | 1 | 1 | 1 | 1 | 1 | 4 | 3 | 5 | 4 |
| I 16 / 152 | 4 | 3 | 4 | 3 | 3 | 5 | 4 | 6 | 6 | 8 | 7 |
| La 5 | 6 | 5 | 7 | 6 | 6 | 7 | 6 | 9 | 6 | 8 | 6 |
| Be2 | 2 | 1 | 3 | 2 | 2 | 2 | 2 | 4 | 4 | 5 | 4 |
| IL-2 | 4 | 3 | 5 | 4 | 4 | 4 | 4 | 5 | 6 | 7 | 7 |
| IL-4 | 2 | 2 | 3 | 2 | 2 | 3 | 2 | 4 | 6 | 7 | 7 |
| LaGG-3 | 3 | 3 | 5 | 4 | 4 | 5 | 4 | 8 | 7 | 8 | 8 |
| MiG 3 | 3 | 4 | 6 | 5 | 5 | 5 | 5 | 8 | 6 | 8 | 7 |
| Pe2  Pe3 | 4 | 3 | 5 | 4 | 4 | 5 | 4 | 8 | 6 | 8 | 7 |
| SB-2 | 3 | 2 | 3 | 2 | 2 | 3 | 3 | 5 | 5 | 5 | 5 |
| Yak-7 | 4 | 3 | 5 | 4 | 4 | 5 | 4 | 8 | 8 | 9 | 7 |
| Yak-9 | 5 | 5 | 7 | 6 | 6 | 7 | 6 | 9 | 9 | 9 | 9 |

| ALLIED | MOVE in mm | ATTACKS | GERMAN | MOVE in mm | ATTACKS |
|---|---|---|---|---|---|
| Albacore | 235 | 2 DC, 3 light or 1 torpedo | Ar-196 | 280 | 2 light |
| Avenger | 395 | 4 DC, 2 heavy, or 1 Torpedo | Bv138 | 250 | 2 DC or 6 light |
| Barracuda | 350 | 6 DC, 2 med, or 1 torpedo | Bv222 | 355 | 6 DC or 6 medium bombs |
| Catalina | 260 | 4 DC, 1 med, or 1 torpedo | Bf109 | 570 | 1 light |
| Firefly | 460 | 2 Heavy or 8 rockets | Bf 110 | 500 | 4 Light |
| Fulmar | 410 | 1 medium | Me262 | 790 | 2 heavy |
| Hurricane | 500 | nil | Me410 | 570 | nil |
| Martlet 1 | 460 | nil | Dornier 17z | 385 | 9 light or 4 medium bombs |
| Martlet II | 550 | 1 Heavy or 2 medium | Dornier 18 | 230 | 1 Arial DC |
| P-40 | 500 | 1 Light | Dornier 24 | 280 | 2 Arial DC |
| Seafire | 515 | 1 Light | Dornier 217 | 400 | 8 medium or 4 Heavy or Fritz X |
| Sea Hurricane | 500 | nil | Fw190A3 | 570 | 2 medium |
| Swordfish | 200 | 3 DC, 2 medium or 1 torpedo | Fw190D9 | 625 | 2 medium or 1 heavy |
| Sunderland | 310 | 4 A DC | Fw200 Condor | 350 | 6 Light or1 or 2 Fritz X |
| Walrus | 200 | 1 A DC | Heinkel 111 | 340 | 7 Medium or 2 torps or Fritz X |
| I-15 | 480 | 1 light bomb | He115 | 380 | 4 medium bombs or 1 torpedo |
| Yak-7 | 500 | 1 light bomb | He 177 | 440 | 9 medium bombs or 2 Fritz X |
| Be2 | 200 | 2 DC or Med bomb | He219 | 605 | nil |
| IL-2 | 380 | 1 medium or 2 light | Ju52 | 240 | nil |
| IL-4 | 390 | 9 light or 5 medium, or 1 torp | J u86 | 350 | High level reconnaissance |
| LaGG-3 | 350 | 2 light | Ju87 Stuka | 370 | 1 Heavy |
| MiG 3 | 600 | 1 light | Ju88A | 400 | 4 Light |
| Pe2 Pe3 | 485 | 2 heavy or 4 medium | Ju88C | 450 | nil |
| SB-2 | 410 | 5 light or 2 medium bombs | Ju188 | 480 | 6 medium or 3 heavy bombs |
| Yak-9 | 530 | 1 medium | Ju290 | 410 | 7 medium or 2 Fritz X |

## CONTROL OF FIRE and FLOODING   Roll D10

| MINOR FIRE | | SERIOUS FIRE | | MAJOR FIRE | | CRITICAL FIRE | |
|---|---|---|---|---|---|---|---|
| 1-5 | Extinguished | 1-3 | Extinguished | 1-2 | Extinguished | 1 | Extinguished |
| 6-9 | Still minor | 4-6 | Reduced to minor | 3-4 | Reduced to minor | 2-3 | Reduced to minor |
| 0 | Secondary explosion Fire becomes serious | 7-9 | Remains serious | 5-7 | Reduced to serious | 4-5 | Reduced to serious |
| Ship may continue to fight and move as normal. No loss of systems or Floatation | | 0 | Secondary explosion Fire becomes major. | 8-9 | Remains major. | 6-7 | Reduced to major |
| | | Ship must reduce speed to ten knots or less to extinguish fire. Can still engage the enemy | | 0 | Secondary explosion. Fire becomes critical. All tankers and ammunition ships explode and sink | 8-9 | Remains critical All tankers and ammunition ships explode and sink |
| MINOR FLOODING & REPAIRS | | SERIOUS FLOODING | | Ship stops to fight fires. Can defend if attacked. May not carry out offensive actions | | 0 | Secondary explosions. Out of control. Ship must be abandoned tankers and ammunition ships explode and sink |
| 1-6 | Controlled / repaired | 1-4 | Controlled | | | | |
| 7-9 | Still minor flooding Repair not completed | 5-7 | Reduced to minor | MAJOR FLOODING | | A ship fighting critical fire may not use its weapons and must remain stationary | |
| 0 | Flooding becomes serious Repair not completed | 8-9 | Remains serious | 1-6 | Controlled | CRITICAL FLOODING | |
| | | | | 7-8 | Flooding reduced to serious | 1-6 | Controlled |
| Ship can continue with normal functions during minor flooding and most repairs | | 0 | Flooding becomes major | 9 | Flooding remains major | 7-9 | Flooding reduced to major |
| | | | | 0 | Flooding becomes critical | 0 | Flooding remains critical |
| | | Ship can continue with normal functions during serious flooding | | Ship must slow to half speed or less while controlling major flooding | | Ship must come to a stop to controlling critical flooding | |

| Cross off 1 floatation box for Minor flooding | DAMAGE FROM FIRES |
|---|---|
| 2 for serious flooding | Cross off 1 floatation box for serious fire. 1 Knot speed loss due to engineering damage |
| 4 for major flooding | Cross off 2 floatation boxes for major fire. 2 knots speed loss due to engineering damage |
| 8 for Critical flooding | Cross off 3 floatation boxes for critical fire. 3 knots speed loss due to engineering damage |

**NOTE** damaged ships can be scuttled with depth charges. A small pattern is expended. Damage is rolled for as if it was a torpedo hit

**HELPING TO FIGHT FIRES**
Warships can go alongside burning ship and help to fight fires on board. If this is the case reduce the die roll by 1 by night and by 2 by day.
It was very difficult for an escort to keep station and fight fires by night, but far easier by day.
Remember that at night any ship attempting to assist another will be lit up by the fires and could become a much easier target for any lurking U Boat. Add 2 to all torpedo chances to hit.
Should an escort be alongside a ship that explodes and sinks, treat it as a torpedo hit.
If a ship is alongside another ship that suffers a secondary explosions roll for damage on the gunnery chart, 4.7" gun column

**DAMAGE CONTROL**
The control of damage was important. Fire and flooding could finish a ship off unless brought under control. Sometimes ever the best of effort failed and the situation grew worse.
The damage control chart attempts to reflect this. Ships generally have a higher chance to totally control a situation, the less serious the damage is. The more serious, the less chance they have. For example a critical fire has more chance of being reduced to a lower level, than it does of being put out completely.
Fire on board ship in a convoy was likely to give away the position of the whole group, not just the ship affected. The status of such ships was therefore very important. It may come about that the player who is senior officer of the escort SOE, decides its better to finish off a damaged ship that continues to burn. Similarly he may decide that standing by one that is gradually flooding is also not worthwhile. Therefore he can order ships abandoned and allow the process of fire or flooding to take its course. Or he may decide to put an end to things and give the ship its coup de grace with gunnery, depth charges or torpedoes

**REPAIRS** Ships can suffer various damages such as electronics and machinery that need to be repaired. These tested on the MINOR FLOODING AND REPAIRS column

## GUNNERY DAMAGE

| | | | |
|---|---|---|---|
| A | One gun mount or Gun director KO. Roll for which | N | Electronics. Wireless/signal bridge hit. K.O. Second hit = TBS KO. 3rd Hit = visual signals KO |
| B | Secondary gun mount KO. (May reduce long range AA) | O | ASW system KO. Roll for which. Roll D 10. Score of 1 = detonation, fatal damage and ship sinking |
| C | AA hit. Reduce AA value by two | P | Torpedo mount knocked out. Roll for which |
| D | Magazine hit. Roll D10. 1-3 = Fwd magazine flooded. 4-6 = Aft magazine flooded. 7-9 central or secondary magazines flooded. 0 = Magazine detonation Ship blows up. If flooded appropriate guns are out of action & major flooding. If flooded can't detonation | Q | Hangar. If carrier there may be more than one hangar. Roll 2 D10 for the percentage of aircraft lost. Critical fire |
| E | Vitals. Roll D10. 1.2.3.4. = power lost to fwd guns. .5.6.7.8 = aft guns until repaired. + Critical flooding 10 knots speed loss. | R | Catapult. Aircraft catapult K.O. If aircraft 1 destroyed. Serious fire |
| F | BRIDGE HIT. Steering damaged. Out of control port 1.2.3.4. Starboard 5.6.7.8. Or Ahead 9.0. Major flooding | S | Minor fire on upper deck amidships. Reduce AA value by one |
| G | NEAR MISS. Engineering. 1 knot speed loss | T | Serious Fire on upper deck amidships. Reduce AA value by three |
| H | Engineering damage.3 knots speed loss | U | Minor flooding |
| I | Engineering damage 5 knots speed loss | V | Serious flooding |
| J | Engineering damage. Speed restricted to half original speed | W | Major flooding |
| K | Engineering damage. Ship comes to a stop until repaired | X | Critical flooding forward. Engineering damage. Can't steam. Can be towed by the stern only |
| L | Power supply damage. All Radar, sonar, searchlights, lose power until repaired | Y | Critical flooding aft. Ship comes to a stop. Can be towed. |
| M | Electronics. Roll D10. 1.2= gunnery radar. 3.4=surface radar. 5.6 = air warning radar. Unable to be repaired | Z | Fatal hull damage. Ship sinks rapidly |

### WW2 BATTLESHIPS BBA (Battleships built between the wars or during WW2)

| | MG | LAA strafe | 3"-4.1 | 4.7" 5" | 5.5" 5.25" | 6" 6.1" | 7.1" 7.5" | 8" 9.4 | 11"-12" | 13" 12.6" | 14" 13.5" | 15" | 16" | 18" |
|---|---|---|---|---|---|---|---|---|---|---|---|---|---|---|
| 1 | | | | | | | S | S | G | G | G | G | G | G |
| 2 | | | | | | | B | BC | BC | A | AC | AC | ACC | ABC |
| 3 | | | | | | | G | G | BC | CF | CF | CF | CF | CF |
| 4 | | | | | | | B | B | BC | BC | BC | BC | BC | BBC |
| 5 | | | | | | | R | R | CR | RU | RV | RV | RV | RW |
| 6 | | | | | | | L | N | BC | BC | BCV | BCV | BCV | BCW |
| 7 | | | | | | | C | U | V | HU | CH | CH | CH | IC |
| 8 | | | | | CS | B | B | V | CG | BH | BI | BI | BCI |
| 9 | | | C | C | B | BC | NBC | LN | LN | LN | EL | EL | EL |
| 0 | C | C | CS | CS | R | T | T | F | E | E | D | D | D |

### BATTLESHIPS Protection class BBM (Modernized battleship)

| | MG | LAA strafe | 3"-4.1 | 4.7" 5" | 5.5" 5.25" | 6" 6.1" | 7.1" 7.5" | 8" 9.4 | 11"-12" | 13" 12.6" | 14" 13.5" | 15" | 16" | 18" |
|---|---|---|---|---|---|---|---|---|---|---|---|---|---|---|
| 1 | | | | | | | S | S | G | G | G | G | CG | CG |
| 2 | | | | | | | B | BC | BC | A | ACC | AB | ABC | ABBC |
| 3 | | | | | | | G | G | BC | CF | CCF | BCF | ACF | ACF |
| 4 | | | | | | | B | B | BC | BC | BCC | BBC | BBC | BBC |
| 5 | | | | | | | R | R | CR | RU | RW | CRW | CRW | CRW |
| 6 | | | | | | | L | N | BC | BC | BCW | BBW | BCW | BBW |
| 7 | | | | | | C | C | V | V | HU | HCC | CHS | BCI | BCI |
| 8 | | | | | C | CS | B | BC | V | CG | BHS | BJM | BJL | BBCJ |
| 9 | | | C | C | B | BC | NBC | LN | LN | LNU | CEM | BE | BEL |
| 0 | C | C | CS | CS | R | BT | BT | E | E | D | D | D | D |

| | MG | LAA strafe | 3" 4" | 4.7" 5" | 5.5" 5.25" | 6" 6.1" | 7.1" 7.5" | 8" 8.2" | 11"-12" | 12.6" 13" | 13.4"14"15" | 16"18" |
|---|---|---|---|---|---|---|---|---|---|---|---|---|
| **BB (older Battleships with limited modification) and BATTLECRUISERS** ||||||||||||
| 1 | | | | | | | S | T | CG | CG | H | H |
| 2 | | | | | | | B | BCC | AC | AB | ABC | ABI |
| 3 | | | | | | | G | H | BC | ACF | ACCF | ABCF |
| 4 | | | | | | | B | B | BB | BBC | BBCC | ABCC |
| 5 | | | | | | C | R | R | BCR | BRU | BCRW | BCRW |
| 6 | | | | | | C | L | LN | BCC | BBCW | BBCW | BBCW |
| 7 | | | | | C | CS | CU | BCV | W | HW | BCH | BCHS |
| 8 | | | | C | C | CS | BU | BCC | W | CJ | BKMQ | BKMQ |
| 9 | | | C | C | C | BT | BCU | NBBC | LNJ | LMN | CEM | CCEM |
| 0 | | C | C | CS | CS | R | BTU | BBT | D | D | D | D |
| **CRUISERS With Heavy Cruiser level protection. (CA)** ||||||||||||
| 1 | | | | | | A | AC | AB | ABC | | ABB | |
| 2 | | | | | | CC | CU | BCU | BCV | | ABCV | |
| 3 | | | | CC | BC | BU | HU | GEU | HFU | | IFV | |
| 4 | | | | CU | BU | BV | BV | AU | ASV | | TW | |
| 5 | | | | SU | R | R | RQ | RJ | CRJ | | BQV | |
| 6 | | | | L | L | I | IV | GU | CGU | | VI | |
| 7 | | | | N | M | CQ | H | HU | GUC | | IVCC | |
| 8 | | | | U | CU | CU | HU | HV | HVC | | JWB | |
| 9 | | | B | F | F | FC | FC | FBC | FVC | | EW | |
| 0 | | C | C | BT | CQ | H | BCT | D | D | | D | |
| **CRUISERS With Light Cruiser level protection. (CL)** ||||||||||||
| 1 | | | | B | A | A | AC | ABC | ABB | | ABV | |
| 2 | | | | B | B | AC | CU | ABU | ABCV | | ABCV | |
| 3 | | | | CC | BC | BU | GU | GEV | IFU | | IFV | |
| 4 | | | | CU | BU | BV | BU | AV | TV | | ATW | |
| 5 | | | | SU | R | RH | RI | RJW | CRU | | ACQW | |
| 6 | | | | G | H | I | IU | GV | VH | | WBBC | |
| 7 | | | B | H | H | H | H | HV | IUC | | HVCC | |
| 8 | | | H | U | CU | CU | HU | HW | JWC | | JWAB | |
| 9 | | | S | F | F | FC | FC | FBC | EW | | DX | |
| 0 | | C | C | I | E | E | EC | D | ABC | | DYT | |
| **AIRCRAFT CARRIERS FLEET AND LIGHT FLEET (CV) (CVL)** ||||||||||||
| 1 | | | C | C | C | CC | CC | ACC | | | ACCV | |
| 2 | | | S | S | CS | CCS | CCS | AG | | | AFIV | |
| 3 | | | G | CG | AG | AH | ACH | AQU | | | AQV | |
| 4 | | | H | AG | AH | FH | FH | LMU | | | LMV | |
| 5 | | | CI | CH | CH | HU | HLU | NV | | | NW | |
| 6 | | C | HU | GL | GU | HU | HMU | ESR | | | MEV | |
| 7 | | C | NC | MU | NMU | HNU | INTU | AFV | | | AIW | |
| 8 | | CS | RS | QU | QV | IVM | IVM | XRS | | | XRS | |
| 9 | | CS | AV | RU | RV | IUS | IVT | IVA | | | JWAC | |
| 0 | | C | CS | US | AIV | AHW | AJV | AJW | XD | | AYT | |

| | MG | LAA strafe | 3" | 3.5" | 4" 4.1" | 4.5" 4.7" 5" 5.1" | 5.25" 5.3" 5.5" | 5.9" 6" | 7.1 7.5" | 8" 8.2" | 11" 12" | 13" 14" 15" 16" 18" |
|---|---|---|---|---|---|---|---|---|---|---|---|---|
| **ESCORT AIRCRAFT CARRIERS (CVE)** |||||||||||||
| 1-2 | | | | | | S | S | CS | CCS | CCS | AS | AFH |
| 3 | | | | | | G | CG | AG | AH | ACH | AR | AQV |
| 4 | | | | | | H | AG | AH | FH | FH | CIU | LNV |
| 5 | | | | | | CI | CH | CH | HU | HLU | MU | MV |
| 6 | | | | | C | HU | GL | GU | HU | HMU | CS | ETR |
| 7 | | | | S | C | NC | MU | NMU | HNU | INTU | AHT | AIW |
| 8 | | | S | C | CS | RS | QU | QV | IVM | IVM | WR | XRS |
| 9 | | C | C | CS | CS | AV | RU | RV | IUS | IVT | IU | IWA |
| 0 | | CS | CS | CT | ACS | US | AIV | AHW | AJV | AJW | FJ | YT |
| **DESTROYERS (Large Destroyers (DDL) move one damage left of what is rolled)** |||||||||||||
| 1 | | | A | A | A | A | A | AC | AA | ASU | ACV | AACG |
| 2 | | | C | C | A | A | AC | ACH | AU | AW | ACV | ACHW |
| 3 | | | C | C | C | AC | ACH | ACI | ACV | ACW | CHW | ACIW |
| 4 | | | P | P | P | PH | IPV | IPW | PW | CPW | APW | ACJP |
| 5 | | A | C | S | F | F | FH | CFN | CFN | FNO | AFN | AFJN |
| 6 | | C | P | P | P | HP | CPU | PSV | OPV | COW | COPT | ACOPW |
| 7 | A | P | U | O | O | IO | OV | COV | HPW | CPW | ACPT | ACPT |
| 8 | C | C | U | C | I | CIS | CV | CW | CTW | CW | CKW | CCKW |
| 9 | C | S | C | U | V | W | AI | AW | AK | KX | AFX | DEFK |
| 0 | S | CM | AC | J | JU | JV | JW | DKT | DX | DY | AAY | Z |
| **OLD DESTROYERS   DESTROYER ESCORTS   TORPEDO BOATS   SLOOPS   FRIGATES** |||||||||||||
| 1 | | | A | A | A | AA | AA | AAC | AAC | ACU | ACU | ACV |
| 2 | | | C | C | C | CC | AC | ACU | ACU | ACV | ACU | ACCU |
| 3 | | | C | V | AS | ACO | AC | ACV | ACU | ACW | CHU | CCHU |
| 4 | | A | P | P | P | IPS | JPV | APW | PJ | CPW | APW | APSW |
| 5 | | C | C | S | SU | FC | CFP | CFP | CF | EFN | AFN | AEFM |
| 6 | A | C | O | H | U | PU | CPV | PSW | OPW | CP | COP | AOP |
| 7 | C | P | U | O | W | OV | OW | OV | IPW | CPU | CPS | CPT |
| 8 | P | F | F | F | F | CI | CW | CX | CV | CPV | CPV | FX |
| 9 | S | S | C | AU | AV | AW | AJW | CY | KO | OY | OX | OY |
| 0 | S | CF | H | I | CJ | JM | KS | DKT | DX | FX | FY | Z |
| **CORVETTES  MINESWEEPERS  SMALL ESCORTS** |||||||||||||
| 1 | | | A | A | A | AA | AA | AACV | AAC | FD | Z | Z |
| 2 | | | AC | AC | AC | AC | AA | ACW | ACU | FD | Z | Z |
| 3 | | A | C | C | CI | CIO | ACIV | ACSW | ACU | FD | Z | Z |
| 4 | | C | E | E | AE | IMS | KPW | APSW | PJ | TX | Z | Z |
| 5 | | C | F | F | DF | CFN | CFP | CFSP | CF | TY | Z | Z |
| 6 | A | F | H | H | HS | PV | CPV | PTW | OPW | Z | Z | Z |
| 7 | C | P | I | I | IS | OW | OW | OTW | IPW | Z | Z | Z |
| 8 | P | CT | J | J | FJ | CJV | CW | AX | CV | Z | Z | Z |
| 9 | S | CS | OP | OP | TO | AIW | AJW | AY | DX | Z | Z | Z |
| 0 | T | CF | F | FI | FIP | JMP | KS | DX | Z | Z | Z | Z |

| | MG | LAA Strafe | 3" 3.5" | 4" | 4.7" 5" | 5.25" 5.5" | 6" 6.1" | 7.1" 7.5" | 8" | 11"-13" | 14"-18" |
|---|---|---|---|---|---|---|---|---|---|---|---|
| | **MERCHANT SHIPS VERY LARGE. (Passenger liners etc)** |
| 1 | | | | G | G | G | G | CGT | ACGT | ACGTV | ACGTW |
| 2 | | | | S | S | S | NS | NT | FNT | FNTV | FNTW |
| 3 | | | S | T | T | T | FCS | FCT | FCTV | FCTW | FCTX |
| 4 | | S | S | CT | CT | CN | CT | CT | CTV | CTW | CTX |
| 5 | | S | C | C | CN | CS | CT | CT | CTW | CTX | CTX |
| 6 | | C | C | CN | CS | CT | CT | CIT | CJTW | CJTX | CJTY |
| 7 | C | C | C | FH | FH | FI | FJ | AFJ | AFJW | AFJX | AFJY |
| 8 | C | H | HN | CH | CH | CI | ACI | ACJT | ACJW | ACJY | ACJY |
| 9 | N | HN | CH | AH | AH | AI | AJW | AJW | AKW | AKY | Z |
| 0 | A | AS | AS | AIS | AIT | AJT | AKT | AKTV | AKTV | AKTY | Z |
| | **MERCHANT SHIPS LARGE** |
| 1 | | | | A | AN | AGS | AGU | AGS | AHS | HNSU | NISV |
| 2 | | | N | G | GS | GU | CGU | CHS | CHNS | CNISV | NJTV |
| 3 | | S | C | HN | GU | GNS | HNS | CHNS | CFIS | CNITV | AKTV |
| 4 | | S | CH | CHS | CHU | CHS | CHSU | ACHS | CINS | ACITV | CKXY |
| 5 | | S | HS | HS | HV | HT | HV | AFHS | AIS | CJTV | CCXT |
| 6 | C | S | HU | HS | FHT | FIU | AIVT | AIS | CIT | KTV | YT |
| 7 | C | C | HS | AH | AIV | AIV | CIW | CJTW | FKTW | XT | YT |
| 8 | C | H | AH | FH | CIS | CIV | FIWT | KTW | TX | YT | Z |
| 9 | N | CH | CH | IS | ISW | ITW | JTW | X | TY | Z | Z |
| 0 | A | AS | HS | CTV | ITW | JTW | KTW | Y | Z | Z | Z |
| | **MERCHANT SHIPS MEDIUM** |
| 1 | | | | C | CG | GN | CG | GU | GS | AHT | HNSU | FNISK |
| 2 | | | NS | GS | HS | CG | GU | HT | ACHT | NISV | FNKTW |
| 3 | | | AC | HN | AHS | GNS | HNS | HNT | CCHT | NITV | TY |
| 4 | | S | CH | CHS | CHT | CHS | CHSU | CHT | ACIT | ACITV | TX |
| 5 | C | S | H | HS | HT | JT | HV | FHT | AFCT | CJTV | Z |
| 6 | C | S | H | HS | FHT | FJ | AIVT | AIT | AFKT | KTV | Z |
| 7 | C | C | CHS | AH | AIS | AJ | CIW | TX | AFKT | Z | Z |
| 8 | C | CH | ABH | FHT | CIT | CK | FIWT | TY | TX | Z | Z |
| 9 | N | CH | CBH | IST | IS | KT | JTW | Y | TY | Z | Z |
| 0 | A | AS | FHT | CTW | IT | KTW | KTW | Y | Z | Z | Z |
| | **MERCHANT SHIPS SMALL** |
| 1 | | | | C | ACG | GN | AGS | AGS | NISV | | FNKTW |
| 2 | | | | IN | INS | HS | AGT | CHT | NITV | | TX |
| 3 | | | S | ACI | ACJ | AHT | HNT | HNT | ACITV | | TY |
| 4 | C | S | CH | CIS | CHT | CHT | CHT | CJTV | | Z |
| 5 | C | S | AI | AIT | CIT | JT | FHT | KTV | | Z |
| 6 | C | S | IS | CIT | FJT | CJT | AIT | Z | | Z |
| 7 | C | CC | CIS | CJT | AJT | CWT | AWT | Z | | Z |
| 8 | C | CH | ABI | ABJ | CKS | FWT | KTY | Z | | Z |
| 9 | N | CH | CBI | BJT | KT | JTX | JTX | Z | | Z |
| 0 | A | ACS | FIT | FKT | XT | KTY | Z | Z | | Z |

## Bibliography of books used in studies toward the production of this series on Convoy actions

| | | | |
|---|---|---|---|
| Atlantic Escorts. | David K. Brown. | 2007 | Naval Institute Press |
| Atlantic WWII Naval wargames rules. | Mal Wright. | 1978 | Protector Games. |
| Allied Submarines | A.J. Watts | 1979 | McDonald & Janes. |
| Allied Escort Ships of WW2. | Peter Elliot. | 1977 | McDonald & Janes |
| American Gunboats and Minesweepers. | H.T. Lenton. | 1979 | McDonald & Janes. |
| Axis Submarines. | A.J. Watts | 1978 | McDonald & Janes. |
| Assault from the Sea. | J.D. Ladd. | 1982 | David & Charles. |
| Aircraft and Seapower. | Vice Admiral Sir A. Hezlet. | 1975 | Peter Davies. |
| Aircraft carriers 1914 to the present. | R. Chesnau. | 1985 | Arms and Armour Press |
| Australian & New Zealand Warships | R. Gillett. | 1990 | Doubleday |
| All the Worlds Fighting Ships 1922-1946 | Group authors. | 1980 | Conway Maritime Press |
| All the Worlds Fighting Ships 1905-1922 | Group authors. | 1980 | Conway Maritime Press |
| Ark Royal. | Sir. H. Russell. | 1943 | The Booley Head. |
| Aircraft Carriers of the US Navy. | Terzibaschitsch. | 1980 | Conway Maritime Press |
| Aircraft of WW2 | Kenneth Munson | 1962 | Ian Allen |
| Allied Minesweeping of WW2 | Peter Elliot. | 1985 | PSL Publishing. |
| At All Costs. | Sam Moses | 2006 | Random House |
| A Sailors Odyssey. | Admiral Viscount Cunningham. | 1965 | Hutchinson. |
| A Sailors War. | Lombard-Hobson. | 1983 | Orbis |
| Allied fighters of WW2 | Bill Gunston. | 1965 | Lansdowne Press. |
| Axis Blockade Runners of WW2 | Martin Brice. | 1981 | Batsford. |
| Bombers of WW2 | Bill Gunston. | 1965 | Lansdowne Press. |
| British Escort ships. | H.T. Lenton. | 1974 | McDonald & Janes. |
| British Destroyers. | Capt. D. Manning R. | 1956 | Putnam. |
| British Warships ONI-201 | US Navy. | 1944 | US Navy Official. |
| Battle of the Torpedo Boats. | B. Cooper. | | Pan. |
| British vessels lost at sea. (WW2) | Group authors. | | Conway Maritime Press |
| British Aircraft Carriers | W.D.G. Blundell. | 1960 | MAP. |
| Battleship Barham. | G. Jones. | | William Kimber. |
| British Warship Design. | Various | | Naval Institute Press |
| Battleships of the World. | S. Beyer | 1977 | Conway Maritime Press. |
| Battleships and Battlecruisers. | S. Beyer | 1978 | McDonald & Janes. |
| British Cruisers. | A. Raven. J. Roberts. | | Arms and Armour Press |
| Battleship Nelson. | Ronald Careless. | 1985 | Arms and Armour Press |
| Battleship Design & Development. | N. Friedman. | 1978 | Conway Maritime Press |
| Camera at Sea/ | Various | 1978 | Bay Books. |
| Cruisers of the US Navy | S. Terzibaschitsch. | 1984 | Arms and Armour Press |
| Cruisers of WW2 | M.J. Whitley. | 1996 | Brockhampton Press. |
| Cruiser at war | G. Haines. | 1974 | Ian Allen. |
| Carrier Operations in WW2 | J.D. Brown. | 1978 | Ian Allen. |
| Chronology of the war at sea. | Rohwer & Hummelchen. | 1970 | Ian Allen. |
| Convoy Escort Commander. | Sir. Peter Cretton. | 1973 | Corgi. |
| Channel Dash. | Robertson. | 1967 | Pan |
| Carrier Glorious. | John Winton | 1986 | Cassell |
| Destroyers of WW2 | M.J. Whitley. | 1998 | Arms and Armour Press. |

| Title | Author | Year | Publisher |
|---|---|---|---|
| Destroyers. | Anthony Preston. | 1977 | Hamlyn |
| Destroyer weapons. | Hodges and Friedman. | 1987 | Conway Maritime Press. |
| Dreadnought | R. Hough | 1970 | Michael Joseph. |
| Deception. | Masters. | 1978 | Moore. |
| Die Deutschen Kriegschiffe 1815-1945. | E. Groner. | 1950 | J. F. Lehmanns. |
| Destroyer Escorts. | | 1969 | Almark. |
| Escort Carrier (Vindex) | K. Poolman. | 1978 | Book club associates. |
| Ensign Series. | Various. | 1970 | Bivouac books. |
| Encyclopaedia of Sea Warfare. | U.S. Smith. | 1971 | Salamander. |
| Escort Carrier. | K. Poolman. | 1978 | Ian Allen. |
| French Warships of WW2 | J. Labayle Couhart. | 1979 | Ian Allen |
| Flagship to Murmansk. | R. Hughes. | 1979 | Futura. |
| Fleets of WW2 | Richard Worth. | 2001 | Da Capo Press |
| German and Italian Fighters of WW2 | Bill Gunston. | 1968 | Lansdowne Press. |
| German warships of WW1 | J. Taylor. | 1964 | Ian Allen. |
| German warships of WW2 | J. Taylor. | 1966 | Ian Allen. |
| German Cruisers of WW2 | M.J. Whitley | 1985 | Arms and Armour Press. |
| Gunboat 648 | L.C. Reynolds. | 1955 | William Kimber. |
| HMS Warspite. | S. W. Roshall. | 1976 | Futura. |
| HMS Cleopatra. | Cain and Selwood. | 1970 | Futura. |
| Hit First Hit Hard. | Peter C. Smith. | 1985 | William Kimber. |
| HM U boat. | John D. Drummond. | 1977 | Tattoo. |
| H.G.76 | Mal. Wright | 1999 | Against the odds |
| Hunter Killer. | W. T. Y'Blood. | 1983 | Naval Institute Press |
| Italian Warships of WW2 | A. Fracarolli. | 1978 | Ian Allen |
| Illustrious. | K. Poolman. | 1965 | New English Library. |
| Iron Coffins | Herbert A. Werner. | 1970 | Pan |
| Jager-Gejagre (Hunters & the hunted) | Jochen Brennecke. | 1956. | Koehlers Verlagsgesellischaft. |
| Janes Fighting Ships. | Various | 1939-48 | Janes. |
| Kriegsmarine. | Robert C. Stern | 1976 | Arms and Armour Press |
| Lilliput Fleet. | A.C. Hampshire. | 1964 | New English Library. |
| Liners in Battledress. | D. Williams | 1989 | Conway |
| Men of Coastal Command. | Chaz Bowyer. | 1985 | William Kimber |
| Navies of the Second World War. (Series) | H.T. Lenton. | 1966 | McDonald. |
| Navie Marinai Italiani | Elio Ando & Erminio Bagnasco. | 1977 | Albertelli. |
| Naval Weapons of WW2 | John Campbell. | 1985. | Conway Maritime Press. |
| Naval Camouflage 1914-1945 | David Williams | 2001 | Naval Institute Press. |
| Mare Nostrum | Mal Wright. | 1978 | Protector games. |
| Merchant Fleets in Profile. | Duncan Haws. | 1980 | PSL |
| Merchant Ships of the World in colour. | Laurence Dunn | 1975 | Macmillan. |
| Principles of Naval Ordnance and Gunnery. | US Navy Official. | 1944. | USN official publication. |
| Relentless Pursuit. | Commander D.E.G. Wemyss. | 1974 | New English Library. |
| Royal Naval Warship camouflage. | P. Hodges. | 1972 | Almark. |
| Sea Battles in Close Up. | Various authors. | 1980 | Ian Allen |
| Submarines of WW2. | Erminio Bagnasco. | 1973. | Arms and Armour Press |
| Seamanship. | Nicholls. | 1937 | Nautical Press. |

| Ships and aircraft of the US Fleet. | James C. Fahey. | 1945 | Naval Institute Press. |
|---|---|---|---|
| Seamanship. | Nicholls. | 1937 | Nautical Press. |
| Scourge of the Atlantic. | Kenneth Poolman. | 1978 | MacDonald Janes. |
| Ships at War. | Pat Hornsey. | 1978 | New English Library. |
| Sea War. 1939-1945 | J. Piekalkiewicz | 1987 | Blandford. |
| The Allied Convoy System 1935-1945. | Arnold Hague. | 2000. | Naval Institute Press. |
| The Doomed Expedition. | Jack Adams. | 1989 | Mandarin. |
| The Worlds Fighting Ships. | Talbot Booth. | 1957 | Sampson and Low. |
| The Battle of the Atlantic. | Terry Hughes & John Costello. | 1977 | Dial Press. |
| The Big Gun. | P. Hodges. | 1980 | Conway Maritime Press. |
| The Critical Convoy Battles of March 1943 | Dr. J. Rohwer. | 1977 | Ian Allen |
| The Electron and Sea power. | Vice Admiral Sir A. Hezlet. | 1980 | Peter Davies. |
| The French Navy in WW2 | Admiral A. Mordau. | 1976 | US Naval Institute. |
| The German Navy in WW2 | Jak P. Mallmann Showell. | 1979 | Arms and Armour Press |
| The Golden Horseshoe. | Robertson. | 1967 | Pan. |
| The Neptune Landings. | R. Bassett. | 1972 | Pan. |
| They Shall Not Pass Unseen. | L. Southall. | 1965 | Pacific Press. |
| The Fiercest Battle. | R. Seth. | 1972 | Hutchinson Press. |
| The Italian Navy in WW2. | Admiral M. Bragadino. | 1967 | US Naval Institute. |
| The Great Ships Pass. | Peter C. Smith. | 1985 | William Kimber. |
| The U Boat Peril. | Capt. Reginald Whinney RN | 1986 | Blandford Press. |
| The U Boat Hunters. | Anthony. J. Watts | 1976 | McDonald Janes. |
| The Royal Netherlands Navy. | H.T. Lenton. | 1968 | MacDonald's. |
| The Second World War. | W.S. Churchill. | 1953 | Penguin |
| The Code Breakers. (Enigma machine) | Hinsley & Stripp. | 1989 | London. |
| United States Destroyer operations in WW2 | Theodore Roscoe | 1953 | United States Naval Institute. |
| United States Naval Fighters of WW2 | O'Leary. | 1979 | Blandford press. |
| United States PT. Boats of WW2 | Johnson. | 1978 | Blandford press |
| United States Navy Destroyers of WW2 | Reilly. | 1978 | Blandford press |
| United States Warship Camouflage 39-45. | C. Ellis. | 1971 | Almark Publications. |
| United States Escort Carriers of WW2 | Terzibaschitsch. | 1982 | Arms and Armour Press |
| US Navy Operations in WW2 | Samuel Eliott Morison. | 1948 | Atlantic press. |
| US Warships of WW2 | P. Silverstone. | 1971 | Ian Allen |
| US Navy in WW2 | R. Heiferman. | 1978 | AP Publishing. |
| United States Fleet Anti-Submarine & Escort of Convoy Instructions," | Fleet Training Publication 223A, | 1945 | US Navy Official |
| US Naval Weapons. | Friedman. | 1980 | Conway Maritime Press. |
| US Navy History of Convoy and Routing, | Fleet Training Publication | 1945 | US Navy Official |
| U Boats Under the Swastika | Jak P. Mallmann Showell. | 1973 | Ian Allen |
| U Boat. | Lothar-Gunther Buchheim. | 1980 | Collins. |
| U Boat Command & the Battle of the Atlantic. | Jak P. Mallmann Showell. | 1981 | Conway Maritime Press |
| Valiant Quartet. | G. G. Connell. | 1985 | William Kimber. |
| Very Ordinary Seaman. | .P.W. Mallalieu. | 1987 | Granada Press. |
| Warship International. | Numerous editions. | - | Warship International. |
| Warship Profiles. | Various. | - | Profile. |
| Warships of WW2 | Lenton & Colledge. | 1964 | Ian Allen |
| Walker RN. | T. Robertson. | 1956 | Pan |
| Warship Perspectives. Volumes 1 - 4 | Alan Raven. | 2001 | WR Press |
| 2194 Days of War | Cesare Salmaggi & Alfredo Pallavisini. | 1977. | Windward Press. |

| ADDITIONAL REFERENCES USED | | | |
|---|---|---|---|
| Stalin's Navy | | 2008 | |
| Hitler's Northern War | | 2007 | |
| The Luftwaffe and the war at sea 1939-1945 | David Isby | 2007 | Chatham Publishing. |
| Command at Sea. (II) | L.L. Bond | 2009 | Clash of Arms |

www.ingramcontent.com/pod-product-compliance
Lightning Source LLC
Chambersburg PA
CBHW041533220426
43662CB00002B/49